A Resource Manual to Be Used

Life With Spice

Bible Study Series

Daisy Hepburn

Regal Books

A Division of GL Publications
Ventura, CA U.S.A.

Scripture quotations in this publication are from *The Living Bible*, Copyright © 1971 by Tyndale House Publishers, Wheaton, Illinois. Used by permission. Also quoted is the *King James Version*.

Published by Regal Books
A Division of GL Publications
Ventura, California 93006
Printed in U.S.A.

(Originally published in a different format by Scripture Press Publications, Inc.)

Library of Congress Cataloging in Publication data applied for.

The author and publisher have sought to locate and secure permission to reprint copyright material in this manual. If any such acknowledgments have been inadvertently omitted, the publisher would appreciate receiving the information so that proper credit may be given in future printings.

Contents

LIFE WITH SPICE

Dear friends,

Jesus told us that we are the world's seasoning and we had better be about our business of making life more tolerable about us (see Matt. 5:13 in *The Living Bible*). He added that if we did not include a bit of zest and flavor there would be those who might lose out altogether.

One cold, snowy January morning, my neighbor Sallie brightened my day with a simple gift—a little bottle of seasoned salt. One taste convinced me I'd found a cure for bland food. Little did I know I'd also found the inspiration for a creative ministry among women.

Just as the seasoned salt was used to show me how really good foods could be, Jesus gave me an inspiration for a possible ministry among women who could use some flavor and encouragement in their lives. The idea came from Him, and as the neighborhood ministry unfolded, it was plain to see His hand in it, assembling the ingredients, blending, mixing, and then having the responsibility for its result.

I believe in a Spirit-controlled optimism that defies defeat in the name of Jesus. If the Lord has challenged you to a personal ministry in your neighborhood, be assured He will see you through. If He has begun a good work (Phil. 1:6) in YOU, let this be the start of something great.

Lovingly,

Daisy Hepburn

Part I: THE RECIPE

1. **Gathering the Utensils**
   (The story of the first Life with Spice)

2. **Appealing to the Appetite**
   (Now is the time for a neighborhood ministry)

3. **Getting Organized**
   (What you need to do the job well)

4. **Loving One Another**
   (Keeping in touch with the members)

5. **Communicating Eternal Life**
   (How to present the plan of salvation)

6. **Planning for the Preschoolers**
   (A sample preschool program)

7. **Seasoning to Taste**
   (Adapting the recipe to personal taste)

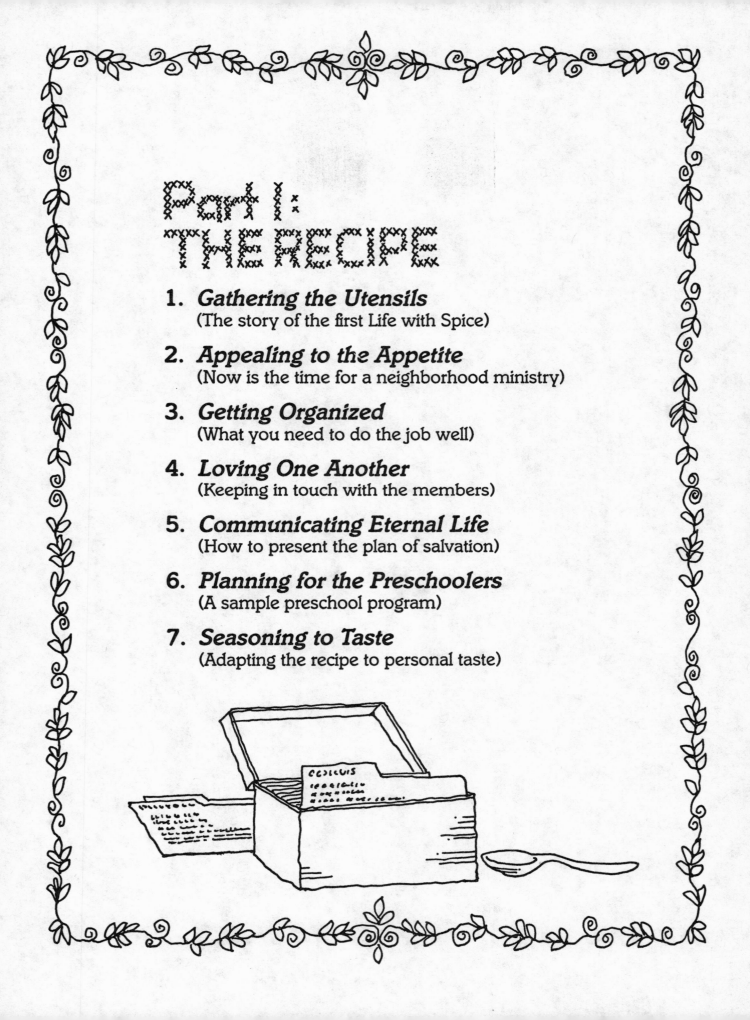

1
GATHERING
THE UTENSILS
(The story of the first Life with Spice)

After the first inspiration from a small bottle of seasoned salt, Life with Spice began to take shape. During a Sunday evening service, an invitation was extended to all women who wished to join in a ministry of flavoring the neighborhood around our church with the love of Jesus. Fourteen women responded and came to a prayer and sharing session.

We prayed that while we wanted to share the love of Jesus, His Word, His plan for our salvation, and an unashamed joy in living, we would also be open to receive what our neighbors might have to share with us.

We were excited to realize that we would use things close at hand and dear to us to build the Lord's kingdom. We would tell our neighbors that we wanted to get to know them because we were all interested in the same things—crafts, recipes, community concerns and, most of all, God's Word.

Definite guidelines began to emerge. We were not forming a new organization in the church. Life with Spice was to be a get-together for neighbors. We would follow the leading of the Lord as to what shape it would take after the first meeting.

We chose the name Life with Spice because we would include several ingredients—with definite variety:
- coffee and simple goodies
- informality
- an activity involving everybody around tables
- a very basic Bible study including a few tools for finding one's way in the Scriptures
- a good, free child-care program.

We prepared and printed a flyer (figure 1). Eighteen women, many of whom had never done any such encountering before, went out on a sub-zero morning to issue personal invitations to sample Life with Spice. Imagine the response when we asked our neighbors to meet us at the church and bring a clean, empty tuna can and a Bible, if they had one!

Fifty-two women responded to that first invitation! They came with their children, their mothers-in-law, their tuna cans and their Bibles. It was difficult to keep the lid on our enthusiasm, but we did pour a cup of coffee and proceeded to get acquainted. Everyone wore the spice jar name tags we provided. One of the most enjoyable recollections of that first morning was the fact that absolutely no one in the room knew every one, and no distinction was made—or is ever made—between the "church women" and the "visitors."

Use a flyer similar to this one to attract women to your Life with Spice. Post them about the neighborhood or, better yet, knock on doors and extend warm personal invitations.

Figure 1

Tuna fish cans never had it so good. One of the women shared the beauty of God's hand with winter twigs and yellow pom-poms. She arranged them skillfully in a little green oasis in the tuna can. Placing a small white rice bowl upside down with an ordinary white saucer on it, the tuna can on top, she created with a few green leaves, three twigs and three bright yellow flowers a remarkable oriental arrangement for a coffee table. It was a reminder that God does care about our enjoyment and appreciation of life and all its gifts.

"Put your arrangement on a pedestal," she said. "It is something very special so allow it to be seen and enjoyed by all who enter *your home*. That is what God does for us—He helps us to know that we are *special*, we are important to Him and that we can have the marvelous fulfillment of being a vessel for His love in the world."

Then everyone got into the act and what fun there was as we tried hard to imitate Bev's simple plan for arranging the bits of greenery. Enthusiasm ran high. Name tags were continually referred to as new names were learned and neighbors discovered one another.

A box of salt was the natural prize for the ice breaker game the women picked up with their name tags.

A former physical education teacher was part of our group, so next we were on our feet to get shaped up. Everyone enjoyed three or four minutes of good, exhilarating exercise.

Our Bible study was introduced and Bibles were given to those who did not own one.[1] After a short ten-minute teaching time, each table group was given the opportunity to have a twenty-minute discussion in conjunction with the outline of Scripture references found in our study booklet. Because of the good fellowship, the welcome, the acceptance, the flowers, the coffee, the exercises, and the availability of the Word, it was evident that we were right to assume that these friends were just as interested as we were in discovering what God has to say to us in the Scripture.

The hour and a half flew by. After the leader brought our study into focus in a fifteen-minute closing application, prayer was offered.

"I'll be glad to bring the treats for our table next week . . . . Has anyone seen a red mitten? . . . No one comes for lunch in our house, so I can stay to help clean up . . . . Shall we leave these cute name tags? I've wanted for so long to get to know the lady next door and I had to have someone point her out to me here, of all things! . . . Never knew the Bible could be as clear as I saw it today in this language . . . . My husband will be so surprised when he comes home and sees the flowers." Conversation at the door was exciting, rewarding, heartwarming and confirming that our concoction had been tasty.

Now, several years later, this first Life with Spice get-together has grown to a weekly gathering of about 200 women. Many, many more have stayed long enough to get the recipe—then have started other Life with Spice get-togethers of their own.

Any group of like-minded women who are concerned about their neighbors can take the ingredients presented in this book, sprinkle with their own seasonings, and stir up a get-together. As stated earlier, Life with Spice is not another church organization (or it need not be). The participants are part of one another and are free to give and receive, thus growing individually by what they acquire together. Combine the ingredients for your Life with Spice get-together to allow the greatest possibilities for personal involvement with the group as well as in preparation for personal involvement with God.

They almost missed her! Soni was weeping behind a closed door that morning in the apartment house complex. Her Air Force husband was at work at the airport near by, but Korean Soni was despairing and expecting their second child. Two neighbors came to invite women to Life with Spice and Soni's door was the last one they came to that day!

Soni came to Life with Spice and understood almost nothing about what was said in *words,* but soon responded to the language of love.

She has a Korean Bible now, a beautiful new son named Jonathan, a host of new friends and, in her own words, "So much, so much, so much to live for." She doesn't seem to be able to stop giving thanks.

Note
1. Bibles and New Testaments may be purchased from the American Bible Society, P.O. Box 5656, Grand Central Station, New York, NY 10163, for a small price.

2
APPEALING TO THE APPETITE
(Now is the time for a neighborhood ministry)

We found that our neighbors were hungry for the same kinds of things that we were. Here is the shopping list you will need:

1. Spices and herbs have become a topic of renewed interest in flavor: *You are the world's seasoning* (Matt. 5:13).
2. Home crafts and creative homemaking enjoy a new popularity as women discover and develop new skills: *To enjoy your work . . . is indeed a gift from God* (Eccl. 5:20).
3. Physical fitness is being reemphasized, as exercise contributes to good health: *So use every part of your body to give glory back to God, because he owns it* (1 Cor. 6:20).
4. Neighborliness and caring for those in your corner of the world are important in a loneliness-producing society: *So we belong to each other, and each needs all the others* (Rom. 12:5).
5. Preschool opportunity for training in the knowledge of Jesus is a privilege: *Teach a child to choose the right path, and when he is older he will remain upon it* (Prov. 22:6).
6. The Word of God has been given to be read, believed, lived, and shared. In the power of the living Saviour, this realization has stirred new appetites: *These are recorded so that you will believe that he is the Messiah, the Son of God, and that believing in him you will have life* (John 20:31).

The following list includes some things we don't need:

1. Flavorless food or savorless living
2. Dull, unimaginative homes
3. Middle-aged spread—or any other kind of spread, for that matter!
4. Isolationism
5. Untrained offspring
6. Spiritual ignorance

This being so, I want to remind you to stir into flame the strength and boldness that is in you . . . . For the Holy Spirit, God's gift, does not want you to be afraid of people, but to be wise and strong, and to love them and enjoy being with them. If you will stir up this inner power, you will never be afraid to tell others about our Lord (2 Tim. 1:6-8).

Now, enrich everything you do with vitamin E:

ENTHEOS="CAUGHT UP IN GOD"
IS THE ROOT FOR OUR WORD
ENTHUSIASM!

Allow yourself the soul-enrichment of a God-administered oversized dose of enthusiasm. This vitamin *E* for Enthusiasm is more than a supplement to your daily diet; it is a minimum daily requirement for those who desire to be the world's seasoning.

The benefits and evidences of the use of enthusiasm shall look different in the life of each woman who avails herself of this energy-producing formula.

But regardless of the form, the demand will increase for what it is that makes you so completely sold on the ministry the Lord has given you.

You will need the following utensils to operate your neighborhood ministry successfully:

People—These are the least you can get by with:

1. A willing-hearted leader
2. A committed Bible study leader (could be the same as 1)
3. Discussion leaders for small groups (ratio 1 to 4)
4. Exercise lady
5. Craft, demonstrations, resource people
6. Greeters and a name tag lady
7. Goodie group—two or three women to keep the coffee perking and refreshments served (everyone takes turns bringing food)
8. Nursery Head to coordinate the child care and preschool teaching program
9. Paid or volunteer nursery ladies

Other tools:

1. *Prayer power* put to the test all along the way! (Please don't attempt to produce this recipe without the most important ingredient!)
2. *Bible study* material carefully selected and made easily available
3. *Table settings* including place mats, centerpieces and coordinated napkins.
4. *Preschool Program* can be carried on right in your own home and with your own neighbors, but the advantage of meeting in a building where nursery facilities are already available cannot be minimized. Take care to provide well for preschoolers. Use of this tool—the training of the tiny—will almost surely guarantee a real measure of reward.
5. *Money* can be collected in breadbaskets or small offering baskets, usually placed on each table. As the craft is shown or the study introduced, the approximate cost is indicated. It has been our *firm* practice to encourage everyone to become involved, with or without sharing in the finance. *The Lord has more than met the need!*

3
GETTING ORGANIZED
(What you need to do the job well)

As you begin to enjoy these mornings together, you will perhaps see the need for a bit more organization. *Under his (Christ's) direction the whole body is fitted together perfectly, and each part in its own special way helps the other parts, so that the whole body is healthy and growing and full of love* (Eph. 4:16).

An extra meeting was called for any who might be willing to take on a special job in our get-togethers. By the use of a Life with Spice Special Abilities list (see figure 2), each woman who wanted to was given the opportunity to become part of the healthy and growing body.

The blanks were quickly filled in and the work was shared and everyone "stirred" up the gift of God that was within them. Because of a population explosion, we have had to regroup several times, recruiting new hostesses to sit at each table. These ladies make certain the women feel welcome, by learning their names and keeping their coffee cups full—then they are willing to lead the discussion time. Each hostess prepares her Bible lesson ahead of time in order that she can make intelligent contributions to the sharing time.

Life with Spice Special Abilities

Read together Ephesians 4:11-16. Here are ways to be part of the healthy growing body:
1. Surely, we can make the name tags and welcome everyone.
   _____

2. I would like to arrive early and get the coffee started.
   _____

3. Yes, I will be glad to recruit and plan the goodies for each table.
   _____

4. I would like to make pretty place mats, table runners or simple centerpieces.
   _____

5. Someone needs to keep a mailing list—ME! _____
6. I will be glad to gather paperback Bibles and keep the supply of study booklets on hand.
   _____

7. Each table needs at least two hostesses. We will become flavorful hostesses:
   _____

8. We will be on the Klean-Up Kommittee!
   _____
   _____

9. The phoning chain would be a good job for me. _____
10. I might be able to take care of the offering and thus pay the bills.
    _____

11. There is a ministry in the nursery for us!
    _____
    _____

Figure 2

4
LOVING ONE ANOTHER
(Keeping in touch with the members)

We knew that if we were to have any communication outside our get-togethers we needed a phoning plan. A pyramid phone plan proved most effective and works very simply.

One woman begins by calling four others who in turn each call four more women, etc., until everyone in the group has been contacted.

Jan, a young mother, was invited to Life with Spice by a neighbor who was a new Christian. Jan had not attended church since her marriage and the study of the Bible was certainly not part of her daily routine. She willingly became our "phoning lady" and discovered that she had something she could do within the Christian community. Jan took her job seriously and in the week-by-week encounters with women who were discovering life in Christ and creativity in Christ, she also discovered that this "phoning thing" was having its effect upon her!

Jan was born again—and her special abilities have been used to glorify the Lord.

It is very important that the women selected for the top of the phone pyramid be responsible, dependable women to insure the message reaching the majority of the group.

The weekly phone call did a number of things.
1. It let the lady being called know that someone was thinking about her.
2. It helped her to remember to come back to Life with Spice.
3. It reminded her to bring with her items for her crafts, her coffee mug and her Bible.

Communication involves more than just dialing a number and repeating a message. It involves caring for the other person and conveying love by listening to what she has to say. It also involves *praying*.

Almost no one objects to being prayed for. Some simple ways of meeting this need among the women who are under the caring influence of Life with Spice are:

- Have an attractive box on each table, into which prayer requests can be placed. Establish a prayer and share time to make known the requests and to pray for them.
- Exchange name tags on occasion for a week or month. Each woman will pray for her partner daily until the next get-together.
- Give several name tags to each hostess who can pray for those specific women during a designated period of time.
- Suggest that the phoners take the opportunity of praying for the woman they are to call just before—or after—the call is made.

You will find a number of ways to make this vital link in the ministry effective according to your special situation.

Almost no one objects to being cared for in a refreshing, simple, and unpatronizing sort of way. Friendship begets concern, concern fosters involvement, and involvement with one another is a natural byproduct of being the world's seasoning. Let the caring happen—the Lord will control the elements involved. There will be questions like, "How will I ever have time for one more person?"

Trust Him even for that!

One way that we could easily see to care for one another and meet some immediate needs is to assemble a grocery shelf. One of the willing women should volunteer a cupboard in a corner of her kitchen in which a valuable collection of cans and boxes of food can be stored. These should be replenished at least once a month by the women of Life with Spice. The volunteer's phone number is shared often and the ministry the Lord will give this couple (her husband should help her in the distribution) will be rewarding. Anyone who knows of a need or is in the midst of a personal emergency can phone and know that a bag or two of groceries will be delivered. Or someone can just stop by and pick it up.

LOVING ONE ANOTHER INVOLVES KEEPING IN CONSTANT COMMUNICATION AND RESPONDING TO NEEDS AS THEY ARISE. Make these activities an important part of your Life with Spice.

5
COMMUNICATING ETERNAL LIFE
(How to present the plan of salvation)

Be sure that you are personally familiar with the plan of salvation and have a firsthand knowledge of what it means to become a Christian, as outlined in the Word of God.

You have received the Lord Jesus Christ into your life as Saviour and want to be seasoning to share your experience with others. Perhaps the following simple outline will be of help to you and to your neighbors in the ministry the Lord has given you. (All references are from the King James version of the Bible.)

1. **God loves you and everyone and has shown this love by sending His Son, Jesus Christ.** *For God so loved the world, that he gave his only begotten Son, that whosoever believeth in him should not perish, but have everlasting life* (John 3:16).

2. **You and I are separated from God and need to be responsive to His love in order to know real freedom from sin and within ourselves.** *For all have sinned, and come short of the glory of God* (Rom. 3:23).

3. **This separation came because of sin, and this sin has a penalty.** *For the wages of sin is death; but the gift of God is eternal life through Jesus Christ our Lord* (Rom. 6:23).

4. **The penalty for sin has been paid through Jesus Christ and His willing death on the cross. No other payment will do or is demanded—not even our efforts at being good enough!** *But God commendeth his love toward us, in that, while we were yet sinners, Christ died for us* (Rom. 5:8).

5. **Forgiveness of sin, and assurance of His presence in your life is a free gift—and it is offered to you.** *For by grace are ye saved through faith; and that not of yourselves: it is the gift of God: not of works, lest any man should boast* (Eph. 2:8,9).

6. **Jesus Christ wants to save you, come into your life and live His life of joy, direction, fulfillment and freedom in you.** *Behold, I stand at the door and knock: if any man hear my voice, and open the door, I will come in to him, and will sup with him, and he with me* (Rev. 3:20).

7. **You must receive Him—and when you do you become His child.** *But as many as received him, to them gave he power to become the sons of God, even to them that believe on his name* (John 1:12).

8. **He has done what He said He would do. Now here are some promises to assure you.** *The Spirit itself beareth witness with our spirit, that we are the children of God: and if children, then heirs; heirs of God, and joint-heirs with Christ; if so be that we suffer with him, that we may be also glorified together* (Rom. 8:16-17; also refer to 1 John 5:12-13).

6
PLANNING FOR PRESCHOOLERS
(A sample preschool program)

Planning child care must be a priority in Life with Spice. This sample outline is given to each of the volunteer mothers who take a turn helping the regular nursery leaders in the 4s and 5s group. Adapt it to your needs and create a similar outline of a job description for all your paid or volunteer leaders. Nursery or baby care will be unstructured but provide nursery workers with lists and suggestions.

Let your nursery help know that they are much appreciated and much prayed for!

SCHEDULE

9:00 Free play—One teacher at each table plays with children and helps them keep materials on the tables.

9:35 Clean up—Sing "This is the way we pick up our toys." Encourage and praise children.

9:40 Sing and march—rhythm band—help children participate.

10:00 Prayer and story—sit with children, helping to keep them under control and listening.

10:15 Memory verse and exercise—join in, encourage children's participation.

10:30 Treats—One teacher at each table talks with children and encourages good manners.

10:45 Craft—One teacher at each table gives individual help.

11:00 Games and/or storybooks—read to group or lead games.

Aim: To love each child for Jesus' sake, to then encourage their love for God, His Word, and songs of praise.

Thank you so much for your kind, gentle, and loving help with these precious children—each a gift from God. It is our highest privilege to be trusted with their care and teaching!

7
SEASONING TO TASTE
(Adapting the recipe to personal taste)

In adapting Life with Spice to your neighborhood, there are so many things to do—and a few DON'TS

DO . . .
1. Choose a neutral meeting place—a church, VFW hall, etc.
2. Set your goal—let it be *friendship and love for Jesus.*
3. Have the very best of nursery facilities and leadership. This is a priority!
4. Keep faith with the time schedule.
5. Give each woman the opportunity to make financial contributions.
6. Use anyone who is willing in some way.
7. Have a simple organization structure, i.e., treasurer, kleanup kommittee, goodie group, kraft kommittee.

DON'T . . .
1. Allow church affiliation to be the deciding factor in choosing the meeting place.
2. Be sidetracked in trying to be all things to all people.
3. Miss the opportunity to teach the children about Jesus and His love.
4. Allow any segment of the program to become overpowering. (This will be a difficult one.)
5. Go into a financial hole.
6. Let the local church women take over.
7. Become denominational or proselytize. It's the Lord's work.
8. Become too complicated.
Do not become controversially doctrinal in your Bible study!

Do present Jesus Christ and the plan of salvation!

TASTE YOUR NEIGHBORHOOD
CHEW OVER ITS UNIQUE POSSIBILITIES
CULTIVATE ITS RESOURCES
THEN
SEASON WITH LOVE
ACCEPTANCE
ENTHUSIAM
COURAGE TO RISK
EAGERNESS TO LEARN

ADD A LARGE PORTION OF IMAGINATION TO MAKE YOUR OWN LIFE WITH SPICE!

Life with Spice is *not* a structured organization within the church. Its strength in your neighborhood will depend greatly on your own creativity and flexibility.

Look over the following five types of get-togethers. Then pray for direction as you try to find the recipe *your* neighborhood needs.

FORMULA 1—EXTENDED PROGRAM

We didn't know how long this idea might be attractive, but we were willing to use it and leave the cut-off date to the Lord's timing.

The first decision was to meet weekly, and it happened that Thursday morning of each week seemed best. You might want to follow this time schedule:

9:15-9:30 A.M. Arrival and settling children in nursery areas.

9:30 sharp! Coffee, tea, punch and goodies are served. Every woman is encouraged to bring along her own coffee mug, which helps the Kleanup Kommittee, and the ecology program!

9:40 A spicy starter—a good mixer to get everyone in the mood!

9:45 Or thereabouts—introduce krafty kreations—usually by placing trays on each table with the materials for that day's creation already counted out.

10:15 Straighten up—pick up—then get up for five minutes of exercises.

10:20 Offer another cup of coffee and listen to general announcements or newsy items of interest.

10:25-10:35 Introduction of Bible Study material by leader

10:35-10:55 Discussion and participation around tables

10:55-11:05 Simple application and conclusion by leader

11:10 Farewell

The hour and a half goes by so quickly, but so much is accomplished. The women will go home a bit breathless, but definitely stirred up!

FORMULA 2—EXCLUSIVE PARTICIPATION

A group of four women had the desire to do something in an inner-city setting, so they went door to door with flyers, inviting the neighbors to a Life with Spice Get-Together. It was discovered, as fifteen women came, that they each had difficult problems to work through.

The original group felt strongly that they should work intensively with the number they had and not attempt to enlarge their scope right away.

In order to make their new friends secure in these new relationships, they asked the women of the church they represented to support these meeting times with their concentrated prayer, rather than with what might be "overpowering presence."

Because of the size of the group, the original quartet was able to work on the grass-roots level in homemaking, visiting in the homes of one another, child care, and even help in guiding the women to social service agencies where needed.

One great day, a visit was made to the pastor of the church, as three of the women had made commitments to Christ and were anxious for some basic instruction in growing as a Christian. It was possible for the pastor to meet with this small group of babes in Christ during the time when the rest of the group was having study time.

FORMULA 3—ESTABLISHED SERIES —Series of several weeks or months

"I just don't think we can make such a long-term commitment."

"My time is already all spoken for—and more!"

"How about a springtime 'getting to know you' project? or fall? or summertime?"

These kinds of responses were made by a small group of neighbors who were anxious to do something to bridge gaps and add spice to the lives of women they had never even met. They lived so close to them, but how could they reach out when each had so much else to do?

A decision was made to have a ten-week series of get-togethers. They placed an ad in the town newspaper and rented the local VFW hall.which had excellent nursery facilities.

A ten-week introductory course on the book of John was begun, complete with coordinating ideas for centerpieces, crafts, etc. Women began to appreciate one another, to visit, to learn, to create, and above all, to begin a whole new relationship with the Lord Jesus and His Word.

At the final meeting they announced that another series would begin in the fall! (At this writing, three sessions have been held with each more effective than the last—the original meeting place will not hold the group—*God has blessed beyond their planning!*)

FORMULA 4~ENDORSED OUTREACH

A church group of like-minded, concerned women is often a unit of the local church women's group. It has happened successfully that such a group has elected to make Life with Spice their special ministry.

Friendship Evangelism—the art of *honoring by listening* to one another and guiding by the power of the Holy Spirit to a vital relationship with Jesus Christ, is a worthy goal for any women's group.

FORMULA 5~EFFECTIVE WORKSHOPS

This design is not necessarily recommended as a beginning. This was used after we were into our sixth or seventh month of meeting.

Things were really humming that morning because a whole new idea was being tried. On that day, the ladies picked up their cups of coffee right at the kitchen window, took them to their tables, were quickly welcomed, and then guided by their leader to the various locations where a workshop had been set up.

Within the group itself, we had discovered many women who had some exceptional skills which they were willing to share. These special crafts required more than one week to complete—macrame, decoupage, candle-making, etc., so all the women were given the opportunity to register the week before to attend the workshop of their choice. They could then enter other workshops for the following five weeks of our get-togethers.

After forty minutes in the various classes, a bell was rung and they reassembled for another cup of coffee, exercises and our Bible Study.

We had a remarkable display of crafts at the end of the five weeks and it served to whet everyone's appetite for those classes they had had to miss. (A second opportunity was given at another time.) Not only was a great appreciation developed for one's own latent talent come to life but also that of the neighbor's. *"Can you imagine that Shirley made that?"*

We used the show-and-tell session as a springboard to other kinds of sharing. We discovered that it became easier for some of the women to express their love for Jesus and for one another after first sharing a bit about their crafts and newly discovered talents.

Some workshop projects might include:

Crocheting
Quilting—and Quilling
Painting—many variations
Candle-making
Decoupage
Wall hangings
Cooking
Needlework of any kind.

The workshop registration plan can be expanded to include interest groups of any sort such as music and singing, in-depth topical Bible Study, sports activities, photography, reader's corner, etc. *This is a great plan for a change of pace.*

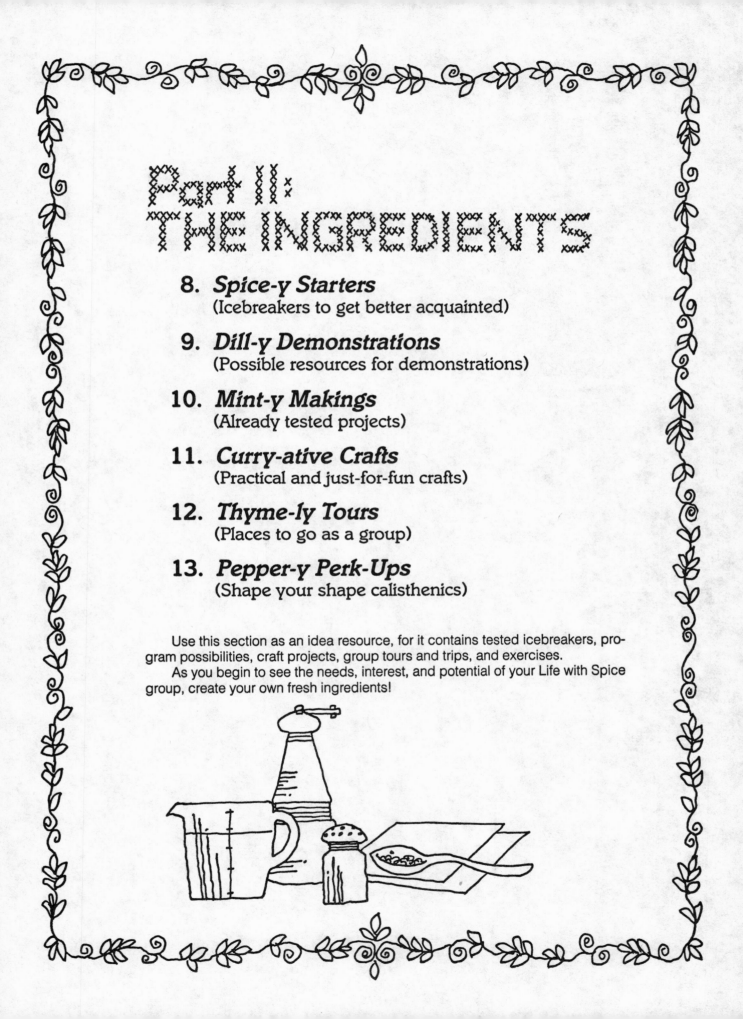

Part II: THE INGREDIENTS

Use this section as an idea resource, for it contains tested icebreakers, program possibilities, craft projects, group tours and trips, and exercises.

As you begin to see the needs, interest, and potential of your Life with Spice group, create your own fresh ingredients!

8
SPICE-Y STARTERS
(Icebreakers to get better acquainted)

A basic ingredient for success in your Life with Spice get-together is a spicy starter or icebreaker to get your group acquainted and in the mood for what will follow.

Be sure to supply materials proportionate to the size of the group. A ratio of 1 to 10 is useful for most of these suggestions. For example, provide a tray of spice samples for each table of ten women.

1. What's in the Purse?
List certain items which may be found in a purse and assign point values to each item (i.e. one point for a gum wrapper, two points for a needle and thread, etc.). Then have each woman check through her purse for the particular items and count up the number of points she has. The woman with the highest number of points wins a prize.

2. Hidden Treasure:
Divide the women into groups. The women in each group look in their purses for interesting articles and decide who has the best. Then group the women with the most interesting articles, and have them share with everyone.

3. Unscramble Spice Names from Mimeographed Lists:
A partial list is found in this chapter. Just mix up the letters in each spice name and see how quickly they can be unscrambled.

4. Identify Unmarked Spices by Their Scent:
Small prescription bottles are ideal to put small amounts of spice in and pass them around for everyone to identify.

5. Macaroni Mix-Up:
Divide the women into groups of ten, seated around tables. Each table is given five souffle cups of macaroni letters. The women pair up and arrange as many names of spices from the letters as possible during five minutes. The letters used are counted and prizes given to the table of participants with the highest number.

6. Have You Noticed?
Before your get-together recruit about ten women to come dressed in some unusual and obvious quirk of fashion. For example, have a woman wear one shoe and one boot, or her blouse inside out, or makeup on only half of her face, or her wig backwards, or whatever else your imagination would allow! At the get-together have these women walk around while everyone is coming in and ask the rest to try to identify both the name of the wearer and her fashion idiosyncrasy.

7. Ad Libs
Attractively mount familiar ads from magazines or newspapers on construction paper and then on large pieces of newspaper, leaving out the actual brand names. Tape ads to walls around the room, then give the women ten minutes to identify the products. Give a prize for the highest number of correct guesses.

8. What's in the House?
Using a doll house (even a Welcome Wagon cardboard box house will do) hide a prize inside. Give a rhyming clue which can be added to each week until the prize is guessed. Qualifications for choos-

ing women to guess might be anything from the one who has a birthday to the one who has the longest run in her stocking.

9. The Price Is Right:
Have the hostess or one other person from each table bring about five articles from her kitchen in a small grocery bag. Cover the prices with masking tape and let the others guess the total cost of the articles. The one whose guess comes closest to the actual price wins a prize. (A possible prize might be the bag of items itself, depending, of course, on the cost involved.)

10. Name that Tune:
There are several ways this might be done. Someone might play on the piano four or five tunes with a specific theme or from a particular era and the women who guess the names correctly win prizes.

Songs with a specific theme, such as nostalgic, modern, sacred, or holiday might be illustrated with pictures (greeting cards, magazines, etc.) numbered and mounted. These should be placed on the walls with a good distance between. The women number their papers, tour the room and try to guess the songs.

Someone who is musically inclined might create a scale by filling glasses with varying amounts of water and then play tunes for the women to guess. Music is available even over the dishpan!

Who would believe a symphony at the sink!

11. Who Is My Neighbor?
Have each lady write her name down on the left side of a small piece of paper, then try to find another person whose name begins with each of those letters. For example:

> D—Doris Smith
> A—Ann Jones
> I—Irene Brown
> S—Sallie Mitchell
> Y—Yvonne Anderson

Each of these other women must sign her paper and the prizes are awarded to the first three who have their acrostic complete.

12. Blindwoman's Bluff:
Try a game that requires using a blindfold. Assemble the following articles on a tray and cover them until the blindfolds are in place. (Depending on the size of the group you will want to provide an adequate number of separate trays.)

Magnifying glass	Battery	Switchplate cover
Flashlight bulb	Wooden match	Eyeglass lens

By touch, have several candidates identify the articles. This is also easily done by putting articles in paper bags and having the women just turn their heads away while feeling the contents of the sack.

13. Candid Camera:
Ask each lady to bring either her wedding picture, her children's pictures, or an early picture of herself. Arrange these on the walls around the room. Allow a short time for the women to circulate trying to identify the pictures. Have each person stand by her own picture to reveal their identity. Use this as an opportunity for each one to introduce herself and her family to the rest of the group.

14. Who's Who?
Supply everyone with a copy of the following outline or any variation to suit your taste and locale. Allow the women time to talk among themselves to find the answers but set a time limit. The woman who fills in the most blanks within the time wins. Be sure to introduce the women whose names are filled in on the winning sheet.

(1) _____ was born in another country.

(2) _____ made a cake from scratch this week.

(3) If given the opportunity _____ would fly to the moon.

(4) I have more than six children (signed) _____.

(5) _____ is wearing more than three rings.

(6) _____ has fixed her own flat tire.

(7) _____ has paid off at least one charge account this week.

(8) "Yes, I've milked a cow." _____

(9) _____ has written and actually mailed a letter this week.

(10) "With these prices, I bake my own bread." _____

15. A Cryptogram:

Reproduce copies of the following cryptogram, one for each lady. Give a prize to the winner.

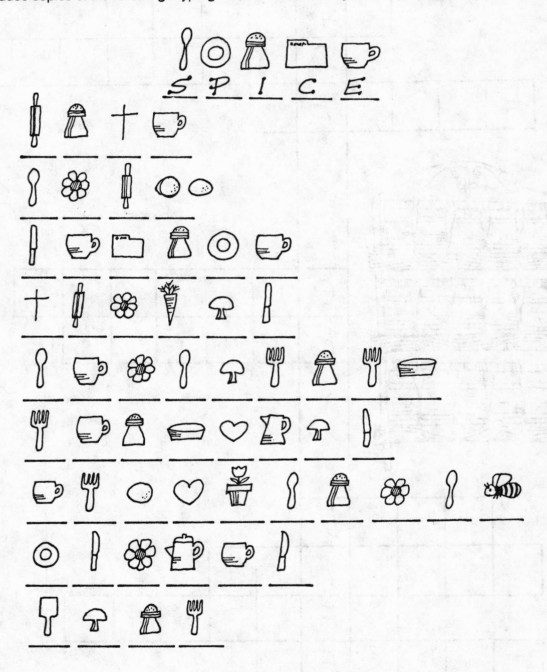

16. Life with Spice:

Herbs can complement many food dishes. However, use them with restraint. Generally 1/4 teaspoon of dried herbs for each four servings is about right.

See if you can fill in the correct letters to complete the names of 10 spices. (Use "F" twice.)

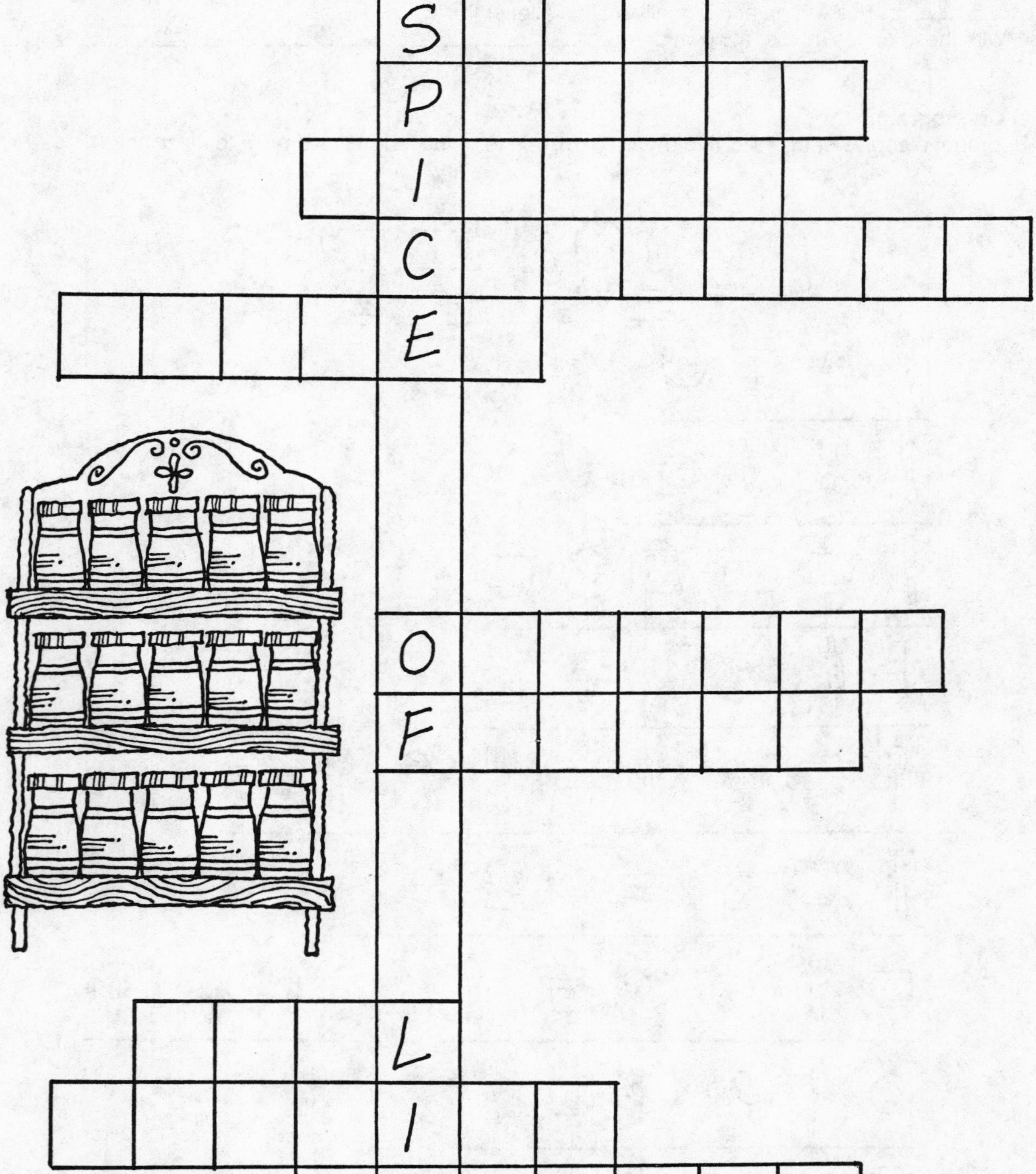

9
DILL-Y
DEMONSTRATIONS
(Possible resources for demonstrations)

1. Large furniture stores sometimes send personnel with instruction and visual aids on interior design.

2. A home economics teacher from a local school might give tips on using color in your home.

3. A drapery consultant from a large department store might be persuaded to give advice on window treatment.

4. The owner of a gift shop might gladly suggest gift ideas for special occasions or un-birthdays and display several gifts from other lands, gifts you can make, or gifts in various price ranges.

5. Check with a county extension service, catering service, or restaurant for a person able to demonstrate some gourmet cooking or candy making.

It was our good fortune to have a visit from the $25,000 Pillsbury bake-off winner who happened to be a neighbor. She came in apron with her recipe and an exciting story to tell about her experience. We had made copies of her recipe and provided each table of women with the necessary ingredients. After her presentation the women stirred up a batch of bars and baked them in the church ovens during Bible Study time. Before leaving everyone had one with a cup of coffee.

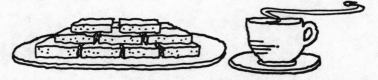

6. Check your group for expert cake decorators, gift wrappers, Ukranian egg makers, flower arrangers, Swedish embroiderers, etc., willing to demonstrate their skill.

7. Invite soloists, pianists, instrumentalists, and groups for special musical performances.

8. Usually antique collectors are very willing to talk about their special finds and show a few choice items.

9. Call your local parks and hospitals to inquire about senior citizen or veteran programs and ask for volun-

teers to inform your group of possibilities for service in your neighborhood. It is *good* to know what people in your community are doing for one another.

10. The telephone company has a variety of programs they're willing to present. Call for a brochure.

11. Gas companies make presentations on a broad range of topics from cooking with gas to conservation of natural resources.

12. A fabric store may send a representative to give advice on patterns or sewing and caring for modern fabrics.

13. Select a pattern and have the women all sew their own variation. Then stage a home-sewn fashion show at your get-together.

14. Depending upon the size and number of personnel at a local craft shop it is often possible to have someone come and demonstrate a specific craft.

15. Someone in your group might prepare a craft in several stages and explain how it's done.

16. Contact your local library for a listing of films available for rent.

17. Hairdressers or beauticians might give demonstrations on hair styles or cosmetics.

10
MINT-Y MAKINGS
(Already tested group projects)

Some suggestions for group projects that have been tested with success:

1. Have everyone bring a clean tuna can and, with some instruction, create a tiny flower arrangement for kitchen or coffee table.

2. Have everyone bring seven cups of flour and, with instruction plus a few other provided ingredients, make bread to bring home and bake.

3. Divide the women into groups around tables. Place several ingredients on each table (with a bit of fore-thought) and have the women make something (without a recipe, of course!) to be baked in the church ovens and eaten together after Bible study.

4. View a short, free film on prevention of home accidents and assemble new first aid kits for their kitchens.

5. View a free film from the telephone company and make prayer reminders by sharing names and phone numbers which can be magnetized and kept on the refrigerator. Perhaps these can be used to form a simple prayer-telephone chain.

6. Prepare 5-inch squares of print material with needles and embroidery thread. Have each woman embroi-der her name and whatever decoration she would like on the square. Join these together making a quilt or large pillow for a neighbor or nursing home resident.

7. Make a *Daisy Pin Cushion* (figure 3).

8. *Fruit Basket Upset*
   Everyone is asked to bring something she is willing to give away. These items should be wrapped. One can of fruit cocktail is purchased for each table and wrapped. Ask the hostesses to bring the fruit cock-tail.
   (1) As the women assemble, all the gifts including the fruit cocktail are placed in the center of each table.
   (2) The day begins with some demonstrations on the uses of fruit cocktail.

(3) The hostess at the end of each table is number one, as the ladies are each numbered around the table. She chooses one of the gifts from the center of the table and opens it. Number two is given the option of choosing a gift from the center of the table or taking number one's opened gift. If she takes number one's, then number one can choose a new gift from the center. After all ten women have had a choice, number one is allowed to make one more decision choosing any of the other nine or keeping what she already has.

(4) This whole "Chinese Auction" occurs simultaneously as each table moves through the hilarity. The closing announcement is made that the one holding the fruit cocktail should transform it into goodies for the next get-together.

9. You might want to decorate *switchplate covers.* Let your imagination by your guide—paint an inexpensive switchplate cover: add bits of pictures, rick rack, macaroni letters, sculptured dough figures, bindings, even ruffles—then varnish for permanence. Make one for each room in the house!

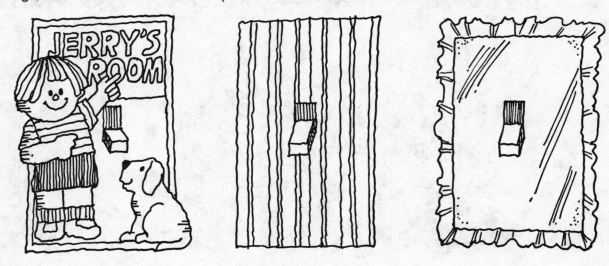

10. A simple, yet always welcome, favor is to take the paper tube from the center of paper towels or tissue, cut into 2-inch segments. With pretty colored 6-inch square tissues, roll the cardboard circle in the center of the square and twist on the one end. Put three or four pieces of wrapped candy into the tissue, then twist the top. Add a Scripture seal on the front or a holiday sticker. Be sure to include some with dietetic candy and indicate which they are before delivering them.

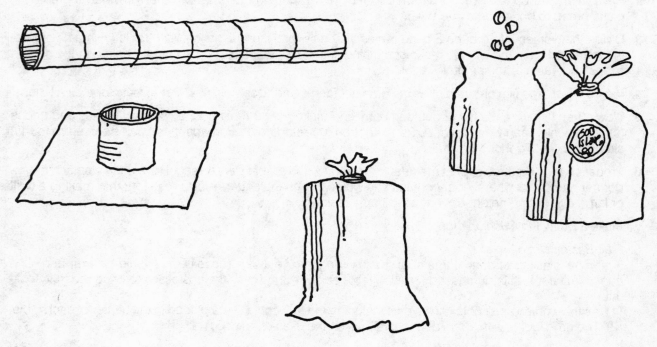

Daisy Pin Cushion

Materials:
  3-inch clay flower pot (available at nursery or garden center)
  2-inch Sytrofoam ball
  Bits of white, yellow, green, and brown felt
  A 4- or 5-inch pencil or dowel

Cut the Styrofoam ball in two. Cover half with yellow felt. Glue the white felt daisy petals to the flat back. Cover the other half with brown felt. Insert the brown half flat side down into flower pot for dirt. Cover pencil or dowel with green felt for stem. Glue two green felt leaves in place at base. Poke blossom into stem and stem into dirt. Either brown dirt or yellow daisy center is the pin cushion.

Figure 3

11
CURRY-ATIVE CRAFTS
(Practical and just-for-fun crafts)

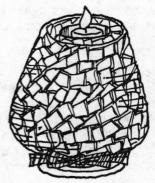

1. Life-with-Spice Plaque:

Take a small board about five-by-seven inches in size, sand it, and stain it. Nail the ring from the top of a soft drink can to the back for a hanger. Cut a picture from a card with a *kitchen* or *harvest scene* and glue it to the board. Using alphabet macaroni print "You are the World's Seasoning, Matthew 5:13" across the bottom of the picture.

2. A Spoon to Hang:

Have everyone bring a wooden spoon. Stain it at the get-together. Place floral clay in the bowl of spoon and stick in tiny straw flowers. Tie a fabric ribbon, cut with pinking shears, to spoon handle in a bow. Screw a small hook into end of spoon for a clever kitchen hanging.

3. Kitchen Bulletin Board:

Cover a piece of thick cardboard with burlap and fit into an old picture frame to assemble a quaint new bulletin board for your kitchen.

4. Stained-Glass Candle:

Take a large bowl-shaped glass and glue a small baby food jar inside to the bottom with Duco Cement. Break other glass jars of various colors into small pieces. After smearing Duco Cement on the inside of the glass and the outside of the small glass jar fill the space between with the pieces. Place a votive candle in the baby food jar. When the wick is lit the candle will shine through the colored glass giving the effect of stained glass.

5. Gingham Flowers:

Take a chenille stem or piece of covered wire about 10 inches in length and form into the shape of petal you want, leaving a length of wire for the stem. Squirt Elmer's Glue along one side of the pipe cleaner. Lay the glued side down on a piece of gingham material and cut around the petal. When you have made four or five petals, hold them together and wrap florist tape around the stems. Glue a pom-pom in center of flower. Felt leaves may be added as tape is wound.

6. Medicine Plaque:

Take a long narrow board, stain it, and attach a hanger to the back. Using colored pills, capsules like red and green Dynamints, vitamins, and aspirin print the verse

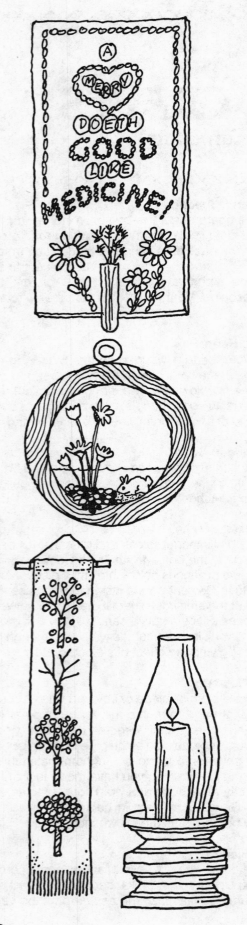

"A merry heart doeth good like a medicine" down the front. Attach a test tube to hold a small bouquet of straw flowers. Hang it in your bathroom next to the medicine chest.

7. Customized Soap:
Take a bar of soap and glue pictures from gift wrap or greeting cards onto soap. Dip the picture into hot paraffin and let it dry a minute or two. This soap can be used. The picture will last through the life of the soap.

8. Spice Rope:
Cut five circles each 6 inches in diameter from printed material with a pinking shears. Place a different spice and a cotton ball (for body) in the center of each circle and tie up in little bundles. Take a 24-inch piece of macramé rope and tie each bundle in a knot along the length of rope.

9. Mini-Pictures:
Paint or stain wooden drapery rings. Glue on a backing cut from burlap, felt, or colored tag board. Decorate with straw flowers, tiny shells, little chunks of charcoal, small twigs, pieces of pinecone, seeds, miniature mushrooms and animals (available at craft outlets) or pictures cut from greeting cards.

10. Clothespin Dolls:
Make rag dolls, tin soldiers, fairy princesses, angels, or little girls and boys. Take regular old-fashioned wooden clothespins (not the snappy type) and paint faces on the heads. Using scraps of fabric, tin foil, lace, chore boys, yarn, pom-poms, bits of leather and whatever else you can imagine, and dress them. Tie a thread around their necks and hang them on your Christmas tree.

11. Four-Season Spice Trees:
Make a wall-hanging from a long, narrow strip of burlap fringed around the edges. Turn under an inch at the top and glue it down to form a casing. Pass a short dowel through the casing and tie either end with a length of yarn for a hanger. Make four trees to represent the four seasons using spices, seeds, peas, and beans. For instance, cinnamon sticks can be used for trunks and split peas for the spring tree.

12. Hurricane Lamp:
Glue four clay pigeons together. Paint if desired. Set a chimney glass on top pigeon placing a large, thick candle inside. Tie a gingham bow around bottom. Stick in a few straw flowers.

13. 3-D Picture:
Sand and stain a piece of wood. From gift wrap cut three copies of a matching design. Glue one complete design cutout on wood. To create a 3-D effect cut out portions of design from the other copies and layer them

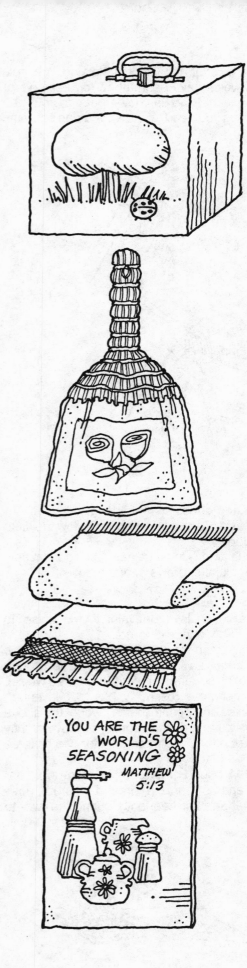

gluing tiny bits of foam or cardboard matchsticks between the layers to give a raised effect making particular portions more prominent than others. Use your imagination in adding bits of fabric, straw flowers, seeds, and moss to enhance the scene. Cover with one or two coats of Modge Podge or thinned Elmer's Glue (three parts glue to one part water).

14. Mini-Mushroom:

Take a small 2 x 2 x 2-inch wooden cube. Stain it, and screw in a decorative picture hanger. Paint in a few bright green blades of grass and a mushroom stem. Glue on a big lima bean for a mushroom. In the corner glue half a yellow split pea. Use a black felt tip pen to mark the head, spots, and legs for a little lady bug.

15. Kitchen Hand Towel:

Cut large terrycloth towel in two—or use attractive terry washcloth. Stitch along raw edge to secure weave. With a *J* or *K* crochet hook, and four-ply washable yarn in a coordinated color, double crochet 80 stitches along raw edge. Chain 2, turn and db 80 back. Db crochet every other stitch. (40db back) ch 2, turn, db every other st (20 back), ch 2, turn, db 10 back, ch 2, turn, DECREASE 1, db 8 stitches, decrease 1 at end of row. Db in eight st for 8 rows. ch 2, turn, db 4, ch 3, db 4 and bind off. Sew button at center of first row of 8 db. Hang on refrigerator door handle or oven or drawer handle or wherever you like!

16. Guest Towels:

Coordinate towels with bathroom wallpaper or curtains or even bedroom sheets by design. Using pastel, flowered, patterned, or bright-colored hand or finger towels add trims, ribbons, and embroidered appliqués. Attach the trim about ½- to 1-inch from the edge of towel by machine or hand sewing and then add appliqués. Decorative materials are available in notions departments or fabric stores. Buy those which are colorfast and machine washable.

17. "Leather" Vase:

Choose a jar or bottle that could be a vase or planter. Take a bottle—wash it, rinse it, and dry it well. Then take a roll of masking tape, tear off little pieces, and overlap them on the bottle until it is completely covered. With an applicator or clean, dry cloth smear brown shoeshine paste wax over the tape and let it dry to give the effect of a "leather" bottle. Use it as a vase for brightly colored dried flowers, graceful eucalyptus leaves or anything that doesn't require water.

18. Decorating Your Cupboard:

Make kitchen plaques by gluing kitchen-type pictures (available often in giftwrap) to a small board, then adding macaroni words from Matthew 5:13—"You are the world's seasoning." Spray completed projects with clear fixative spray.

19. Covered Coat Hanger:

How about covering a coat hanger with rug yarn (since it takes two) for hanging knit clothing. A simple method of buttonhole tying the rug yarn over the two hangers which have been taped together in four places, is easily taught (figure 4). Find someone (preferably someone who has never been to your get-togethers before—thereby letting her know that she has something you need to know) who can show the group how to do this.

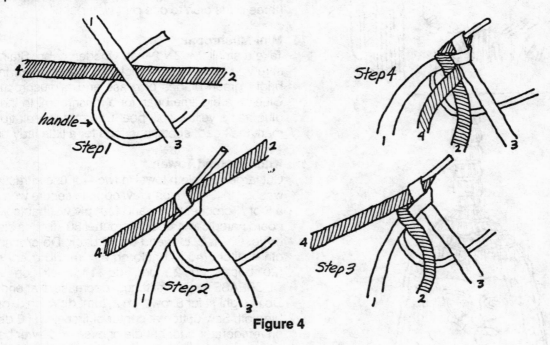

Figure 4

20. Potpourri:

This is a way of enjoying some of your garden flowers and their fragrances all winter long.

(1) You need to dry the flowers by placing them on a screen (such as a window screening) to allow the air to circulate around them. Favorite herbs and spices may be added.

(2) Mix the dried flowers in layers with the other ingredients and seal tightly in containers, giving them several weeks to blend. Then uncover and place the containers in closets, drawers, or a room.

Suggested combinations could be:

a. For a mixed one—rose, violet, geranium, lemon verbena, carnation, lavender, mint, thyme, anise. To each quart add 1 teaspoon of cinnamon, coriander, mace, and 1 ounce orrisroot.

b. For a spicy one—use ½ pound coarse salt, ½ pound common, non-iodized salt, and ½ ounce each of ground orrisroot, nutmeg, cloves, cinnamon, allspice, borax and benzoin. Add 1 cup ground orange and lemon peels, and ½ teaspoon musk. Store in tightly covered jars for two or three weeks.

c. A combination—mix dry leaves of lemon verbena, sweet marjoram, rosemary, bay leaf, lavender, violet, rose and carnation. In a jar place a layer of the dry leaves and petals, then a layer of the above spice mixture; then you continue alternating these two layers to the top of the container. Cover tightly and let it stand for two days, then mix thoroughly from the bottom. Stir frequently for two or three weeks.

d. For a rose one—take a pound of dry rose petals and add ¼ pound of each of the following: non-iodized salt, coarse salt, and brown sugar. Add ½ ounce each of benzoin, ground orrisroot, powdered clove and storax. Store in a tightly covered container and stir frequently during the two- to three-week period.

21. Dilly Dolly:

Head: 3-inch Styrofoam ball
Hands: 1¼-inch Styrofoam ball
Feet: 2⅛-inch Styrofoam egg
Legs: 1-inch Styrofoam pole
Base: 8-inch circle heavy cardboard
Body: 4-inch Styrofoam cone
Dress: 5 x 12-inch piece of fabric

Sleeves: (2) 4 x 4-inch piece of fabric
Bonnet: (1) 9-inch circle of fabric
        (2) 6-inch circle of fabric
* Dip N' Drape (pre-glued fabric)
Hair: 2 x 6-inch piece of fake fur
Glue, pins, gesso, acrylic paints
* Available in craft stores.

To make your Dilly Dolly—(see figure 5)

(1) Legs: cut Styrofoam pole into 2-inch lengths; cover with Dip N' Drape and let dry. Coat with gesso.
(2) Feet: cut Styrofoam egg in half—round edges. Cover rounded part of egg first with Dip N' Drape and then add "sole" to shoe with Dip N' Drape; let dry and cover with gesso.
(3) Hands: cut small Styrofoam ball in half. Notch a piece out to make a thumb. Cover with Dip N' Drape and crease for fingers and let dry. Cover with gesso.
(4) Head: cut a small slice off bottom of ball. Roll the Styrofoam ball along edge of table. Indent ball midway between top and bottom part that was cut off halfway around to make cheek. Soften all sharp edges. Flatten top part to make forehead. Add a nose made from a small piece of Styrofoam—rolled around. Nose should sit on the "shelf." Cover head with Dip N' Drape—pin around nose to keep shape until dry. Give two coats of gesso.
(5) Paint legs, hands, and head with flesh-colored paint. Paint shoes whatever color desired. Paint face: Be sure and set eyes part way down onto the cheek line. Paint black; when dry add two white dots. Use permanent felt tip for mouth. Use toothpick to make freckles (brown). Add two small lines for eyebrows.
(6) Cover cardboard with felt or fabric.
(7) Attach head to body cone with toothpick and glue. Be sure that more of the head is behind neck rather than in front.
(8) Glue body on covered cardboard. Glue legs and feet on.
(9) Dress: cut a 5 x 12-inch piece of printed fabric and a 4½ x 11½-inch piece of Dip N' Drape. Lay fabric facedown on table, cover with Dip N' Drape and spray with water until wet. Fold edge of materials over Dip N' Drape. Gather around the top of cone at neck and tie with string until dry. Pin back of dress together until dry.
(10) Sleeves: 4 x 4-inch fabric and 3½ x 3⅓-inch Dip N' Drape.
Follow directions for dress. Gather top of tube and glue to body to make sleeve. When dry, glue hands in place.
(11) Hair: lay a 2 x 6-inch piece of fur on table; brush it, part it, and then pin around the face—starting at center front.
(12) Bonnet: cut 3-inch circle out of the two 6-inch circles of fabric and one 6-inch circle of Dip N' Drape. Sandwich the *wet* Dip N' Drape between two fabric cones and place on head—bring down in back to cover the neck. Pin a wad of paper towels (two squares) about 4 inches in diameter to top of head. Lay large 9-inch circle of fabric facedown on table and add Dip N' Drape—spray until wet. Center over wad of paper and gather edges. Pin to head all around the paper meeting the brim. Hide all raw edges with trim.

DILLY DOLLIES IN

DAY	PROJECT	SUPPLIES
1	Cover legs, feet, and hands with Dip N' Drape. Dry. Paint with gesso if desired.	Bowl of water for each table; Wax paper, napkin size, to work on.
2	Cover head. Paint legs, hands and feet.	Dish of water Black paint Flesh paint Gesso (if desired)
3	Paint head and face. Cover cardboard circle.	Water for cleaning brushes. Black, flesh, and blush paint. Red, fine line, felt tip pens. Glue for cardboard.
4	Glue doll together using toothpicks to join Styrofoam parts to be reinforced by glue. Make dress from fabric and Dip N' Drape.	Glue; Toothpicks; Bowls of water or sprayers; String.
5	Sleeves and hair.	Bowls of water or sprayers.
6	Bonnet.	Bowls of water or sprayers.

Figure 5

SIX EASY STEPS

EACH NEEDS TO BRING	PARTS THAT NEED PREPARATION
Shoe box; Pins; Scissors;	Cut legs (2 for each); 2-inch Styrofoam pole; Cut feet, cut hands (w/notch).
Paint brush; Pins; Scissors; A shoebox to keep it all in.	Flatten heads; Pour paint into baby food jars for each table; Gesso—if you like— into jars.
8-inch cardboard circle; Fabric to cover; Scissors	
Fabric of their choice; Scissors; Pins.	Dip N' Drape cut for dress.
Scissors; Pins.	Fake fur cut for hair; Dip N' Drape for sleeves.
Ribbon or fabric for bonnet band; Fabric for bonnet; Pins.	Dip N' Drape for bonnet.

22. Bread-dough Basket

Utensils needed:
- Pastry board
- Rolling pin
- Ruler
- Knife or pizza cutter
- Toothpicks
- Measuring cups
- Pastry brush
- Aluminum foil
- Baking sheet
- Shortening or other non-stick product

Suggested forms:
- Cake pans, oblong, round or square
- Loaf pans
- Clay pots
- Tin cans
- Coffee cans
- Bowls

(1) Mix together
   - 4 cups flour
   - 1 cup salt
   - 1-½ cups hot water
(2) Knead for 8-10 minutes
(3) Roll out portion on floured pastry board until the dough is about ⅛-inch thick.
(4) With ruler and toothpick, mark off ¾-inch wide strips. Cut with knife or pizza cutter.
(5) Line outside of bowl or pan with foil and apply shortening. Place strips on bowl and weave pattern. Seal with a little water at joints.
(6) Knead scraps till smooth. Form two ropes and then twist and place on bowl.
(7) Place on greased cookie sheet and bake at 325° for 30-35 minutes or until brown. Remove from oven and then remove from form. Place back in oven for 15-20 minutes till inside is brown.
(8) Spray with clear plastic spray or varnish when cool.

Note: If baskets become soft in time, simply rebake and respray. To clean, wipe with a damp cloth.

12
THYME-LY TOURS

1. Visit a local garden spot in the spring or fall:
There is a university-sponsored arboretum about a half hour's drive from where we meet on Thursday mornings. After a phone call to rent a school bus for transportation we:

- enlist a few women to bring thermos jugs of coffee
- ask another to pick up donuts
- and have everyone chip in for the bus transportation (amounting to about $1.00 per person).

These special two-hour-and-fifteen-minute get-togethers are pure joy! We leave at 9:15, arrive at the arboretum at 9:45, walk through the woods and lanes, coffee in an arbor at 10:20, share some time in the Word, and are back on the bus at 11:00.

2. Arrange a tour:

- to a special food processing plant (tour and samples are available)
- to a spa or health club where guest passes might be provided for a first-time visit
- to a roller skating rink that might be taken over for a mother's morning out.

(All of these and more ideas depend on your locale.)

3. A mystery tour:
Travel to a special spot of interest. Just assemble the women and provide transportation—either in a caravan of cars, or a bus. Then have a short program and goodies. This could be done treasure-hunt style, with various clues placed at different homes, until the final destination is reached. That destination could be anything from visiting the home of one of the women (maybe one that lives some distance from your meeting place) to another Life with Spice group.

4. A tour to a spot for a day apart—for Life with Spicers:
Special studies can be offered in more depth than during the usual time segment provided in your get-togethers. This is a great opportunity for cultivating friendships already formed as well as for leading your women to a closer walk with the Lord Jesus. Provide a good leader or speaker for some group sessions; then add zest with a new craft idea (using perhaps the out-of-doors to provide craft materials); have a lunch served or brought along; provide for child care (either help the women to find home baby-sitters, or have a special nursery day care program at a central meeting place).

Much prayer for these preparations will insure a great day apart—not to "come apart" but maybe to "get it all together" for the first time!

5. Neighborhood progressive walking tour:
a. Ask four or five women—whose homes are within walking distance of your meeting place and each other—to act as hostesses.
   HOME #1. Fixes the coffee and goodies.
   HOME #2. Shows off her newly redone family room (minihouse tour)
   HOME #3. Prepares some icebreaker type game with a prize.
   HOME #4. Shares some recipe from her kitchen and hands out copies to everyone—with a sample!

b. Assemble at meeting place and, if your are working with four homes, arrange your number into reasonably evenly-sized groups, the simplest way being through the use of name tags in different colors or shapes. Each group should have a leader whose job it is to keep everyone moving along throughout the route.

c. Arrange a route for each group so that each of the four groups begins at a different home. After a specified time period—fifteen or twenty minutes—in the home, the leader moves everyone along to their second home.

d. After all the homes have been visited, the walk is taken back to the central meeting place for a time of Bible study and devotions.

When we tried this, it was a trick-or-treating day at Life with Spice. Believe it or not, the women came in costume—some more than others!—and we walked through the neighborhood for just treat, no tricks . . .

I wish I could find words to describe the unabashed fun we had!

Our Bible Study was based on some of the disguises Satan uses and how we have to be on guard (1 Pet. 5:8,9). (Try having the women paraphrase it according to where they are right now.)

6. Day in the country:

One of our women lives about ten miles away from our meeting place on several acres of real Minnesota, country-type land, and she invited the Life with Spice for a fall treat to come for coffee.

We boarded rented buses (everyone adding her $1.00 for cost), and after a twenty-minute ride, we started our autumn walk through a field at the edge of her property. We gathered lots of the drying fall weeds as we walked the trail to their home. After prayer, coffee, cider, cheese, and nut bread was served near the back door from a cart.

A short devotional was so very special in that setting—after which we had some instruction on how to arrange our weed gleanings in paper cups and sand.

The fall dry weed arrangements were brought to the next meeting of Life with Spice and served as table decorations as well as conversation pieces. Some pictures were taken at the country coffee party which were arranged later into a lovely bulletin board reminder of the Thyme-ly Tour.

13
PEPPER-Y PERK-UPS
(Shape your shape calisthenics)

Flexibility is the "spice of life" and that means a flexible you for a life with zest.

One of a woman's problems is her shape. There are over 600 muscles in the body which need exercise to keep their shape. When muscles are not used enough they become weak and flabby—they sag. Extra fat settles around these muscles because weak muscles cannot break up this fat and move it out of the system.

Exercise helps to bring sagging muscles back into tone, and that can help in weight loss. Keep exercising—every day—and your body will eventually firm and tighten, helping you to shape up!

In addition, by correcting bad posture, you can give the appearance of being ten pounds thinner than you really are. So:

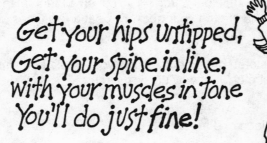

Get your hips untipped,
Get your spine in line,
with your muscles in tone
You'll do just fine!

The Bible says in Proverbs 31:17: She girded her loins with strength and strengthened her arms.

"She diets and exercises to keep herself physically fit." (paraphrase by Mrs. Carolyn Lung)

Do some exercises before Bible Study.

"ALL OVER" EXERCISES–FROM TOP to TOE!

Do these exercises ten times per day for the first week, after that twenty per day:

1. **Head**—stand astride, arms at side. Relax head forward, then stretch head up, with chin in, chest lifted.

2. **Shoulders**—stand astride, cross arms in front of chest, then swing them upward and backward.

3. **Bustline**—stand astride, put your hands together in front of your chest, and push your palms together, hard.

4. **Waistline**—stand astride, hands on hips. Bend forward from the waist up and make a complete circle with your body, forward, side, back, side.

5. **Stomach**—stand astride, arms straight over head. Bend forward and touch your toes ten times.

6. **Hips**—lie down on your back, arms out straight beside you, shoulders high. Bring your knees up to your chest, now roll from side to side, keeping your back flat on the floor.

7. **Thighs**—stand with one side to a wall, and hold on to wall with one hand. Kick the outside leg as high as you can, back and forward. Turn to the other side and repeat. Ten times each side.

8. **Calves**—stand with feet together, toes pointed inward just a little. Do alternate heel raising and lowering, going way up on the toes.

9. **Ankles**—sit on floor, with legs straight out in front of you, one leg crossed over the other at the ankle. Make twenty complete circles with the foot on top. Change and repeat with other foot.

EXERCISES WHILE WORKING IN THE KITCHEN

1. When you are doing the dishes, be kind to your feet! Take off your shoes and stand on the outer edges only, with feet curled outward. Then stand with the toes turned up as far as they'll go.

2. After sewing for a long time, do the shoulder shrug. Pull your shoulders up to the ear level, then press them down; then lift your head and stretch your neck. Repeat a few times and you'll feel tension go away.

3. When you reach for something stored on a top shelf, put your whole body into the stretch; pull in the stomach, tuck in the seat, and stretch your way up on the toes.

4. When ironing, take a break and stand on one leg and bend the other leg at the knee; then raise up on the toes several times. Change legs and repeat.

5. While picking up toys or something light from the floor, make the motion like a toe-touching exercise; bend from the waist and keep the knees straight. When you are picking up something heavy, do a deep-knee bend, and let the legs do the lifting.

6. Carry a light laundry load, anything light and unbreakable, upstairs by balancing it on your head. Keep your back straight, head erect, hips tucked under.

7. When making beds, bend forward from the waist and keep your back straight when you are stretching over the bed to smooth the corners; stretch as far as you can reach before changing your position. When you bend, bend from the waist, with back, shoulders, and knees straight.

8. When you are working at the kitchen counter, place hands, palms up, under the countertop. Push up, hard, as though you were lifting it. Relax, and repeat.

9. During gardening, alternate deep-knee bends with bending from the waist when you plant or weed. Take advantage of the outdoor air and take deep, slow breaths.

10. Before getting out of bed in the morning, or when going to bed at night, lie on your back with your head on a pillow. Try to push your head back through the pillow. Breathe normally, and hold for six seconds.

Part III:
THE FINISHED PRODUCT

On the following pages are some complete sessions for you to try—ideas for get-togethers, banquet programs and a formal luncheon.

They have all been arranged with the basic concept of total involvement, which means living a Life with Spice.

14
SALAD SEASONING

1. At an earlier meeting, write ingredients for a salad on slips of paper: lettuce, tomatoes, cut-up carrots, cut-up celery, etc. Provide enough ingredients for an ample salad for each prospective guest. Put the slips in a salad bowl and have the women draw their assignments for the special salad lunch you will be having at the next get-together.

   Here is a simple recipe for croutons which someone else can bring: In a skillet melt 2 Tbsp. butter or margarine. Toss with 1 cup bite-size shredded rice cereal (Rice Chex, for instance) and ½ tsp. garlic.

   ## SEASONED SALT

1 cup coarse salt	1 tsp. curry powder
1 tsp. dried thyme	2 tsp. dry mustard
1½ tsp. dry oregano	½ tsp. onion powder
1½ tsp. garlic powder	¼ tsp. dill weed
2 tsp. paprika	

   (1) Prepare a tray for each table with cupcake papers containing a sufficient amount of ingredients to make one recipe of seasoned salt for a table.
   (2) Gather or buy enough small capsule vials (plastic medicine bottles) for each woman to receive a good-sized sample of the salt mix.

2. **Set the tables:**
   For place mats use paper towels decorated with kitchen utensils. Put a recipe card at each place.
   As you shop, watch for new patterns of napkins or paper towels, or samples of new products. Remember that you will be able to use them. Create a tiny Life with Spice pantry of goodies to accent your meetings.

3. **Centerpiece Ideas:**
   (1) Bunches of parsley in cruets tied with apple green ribbon
   (2) Parsley or other herb plants with a bow
   (3) A topiary tree:
   Take a clay pot with a 5-inch diameter. Paint it or cover it, if you like. Fill it with just enough plaster to make a 12 x 15-inch dowel stand in place. Sprinkle coffee over the plaster to look like dirt. Stick a head of leafy lettuce, red cabbage or white cabbage onto the dowel and tie a bright ribbon around the "stem."
   (4) For a more elaborate and spectacular centerpiece: Cut out the center of a good-sized cabbage and fit a can of Sterno right down into it so that the top of the can is even with the top of the cabbage. Poke toothpicks with bits of Vienna sausage into the cabbage. When it is time, let the women toast their sausages over the flames for a taste treat!

4. Now You Are Ready!

(1) The ladies arrive and take their salad makings to a central spot so that a few can arrange the salad bar in a pleasant order.

(2) Here is a *spicy starter:*
Provide ten lunch bags, numbered, containing a sample of a different spice in each bag. Pass the bags around giving each woman a chance to smell the spice without seeing, touching, tasting or even peeking! Each pair of ladies, or each table, or even each woman individually must make a list of what they think the spices are.

How about a bouquet of parsley for the winners . . .
Or a package of herb seasoning? Or . . .

Since this is a salad-type day, how about holding up various kinds of lettuce and see who can identify them? Perhaps this could be done collectively at each table. After participants think they know the answer, let them stand up quickly. See how they do and then present each one with a head of lettuce.

(3) A home economist from a local supermarket might demonstrate how to select, store and serve the variety of greens available.

(4) Mix up the recipe for seasoned salt using the ingredients provided on the tray and let everyone pour themselves enough to sample now and to take the remainder home.

5. The Salad Bar is ready to serve and the women can go up and serve themselves in paper salad bowls provided. Have them add a bit of dressing and seasoned salt. It is good to serve rolls as well as the croutons.

Now end your get-together with a bit of soul food:

You Are the World's Seasoning
Jesus summarizes the properties of the world's seasoning in the beatitudes in His Sermon on the Mount, Matthew 5:1-13. Let the women take their Bibles and turn to this Scripture portion. Ask them to find as many common properties as they can comparing salt and the happy people that Jesus is describing in these verses:

- Humble (v. 3) Salt is less than effective if it is too noticeable or overpowering.
- Hungry and Thirsty (v. 6) Salt creates thirst. Happy are those who know a hunger and thirst for righteousness and by whose living a hunger and thirst for righteous living is created.
- Pure (v. 8) Salt purifies. Happy are those whose hearts and lives are pure and by whose presence a purifying element is introduced into an impure world.
- Peacemaking (v. 9) Salt melts and tenderizes. Happy are those whose own lives know His peace, so they can be melting agents in this world. They are happy to show tenderness through the Holy Spirit's power.
- Persecuted, yet preserved (v. 10) Salt preserves. Happy are those who have been tested and kept by the power of God. Now they are able to show others that He does *stablish, strengthen,* and *settle!*
- Think of those you know who exemplify some or all of these qualities.

Notice the commission Jesus gives His followers in verse 13, and His warning if we do not fulfill it. What will happen to the world?
Talk about salt
—its ancient value
—its life-sustaining properties
—its possibility of needing reflavoring.

Are you worth your salt?

(You might want to read Colleen Townsend Evans' book, *A New Joy,* Fleming H. Revell Co., New Jersey 1973, with its commentary on the Beatitudes and being salty Christians.)

15
PATCHWORK PARTY

Preparations:

1. Make name tags shaped like spools of thread.

2. Obtain a tiny sewing kit for each woman as a favor.

3. Prepare centerpieces for each table. They might be sewing baskets with a bunch of bright fabric flowers.

4. Use patchwork gift wrap to make folders or envelopes for dress patterns as the women assemble all the ideas they will gather.

5. Mimeograph or photocopy some actual patchwork patterns.

6. Set your tables with scraps of 12 x 18-inch fabric for place mats, or center tablecloths of just one yard square of calico or print fabric.

At the Get-Together:

7. After each lady has come in, been welcomed, and picked up her name tag, ask her to think about her most embarrassing moment, and be ready to share it around the tables.

8. A little later, each table can award a prize to the woman who has kept the rest in **stitches** most effectively!

9. Ask each to see how well she can visualize her own waist measurement. Give each woman a piece of string at least 1½ yards in length. Each lady will lay it on the floor in a circle—the size of her waist. Holding the measured length tightly, she measures her waist to see how she did. The one who comes closest wins a measuring tape, of course!

10. Bring three dress patterns already cut out and select three models and three pinners, forming three teams made up of one model and one pinner. At the signal, each pinner pins one of the dress patterns to her model. The "sharpest pinner" and model who finish first—with all parts in their right place—wins.

This is a good time for a short, home-sewn fashion show.
Or, a representative from a local fabric store who can demonstrate the contents and care of modern fabric.
Or, a demonstration on how to re-create old colonial patchwork patterns (see figure 7).

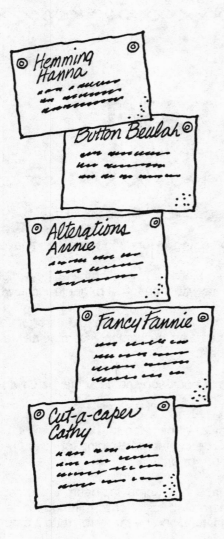

11. Patchwork shops:

This idea can serve as a mixer as well as a few minutes of real instruction.

In several locations around the meeting area signs could be posted indicating where these special workshops are meeting.

Ask your best sewers to share their talent in these simple ways:

- *Hemming Hanna* can demonstrate the proper way to hem a garment. Have some scraps of material, needles and thread available so all can take the tips and put them into practice.
- *Button Beulah* can show good, secure ways to sew on buttons. Then, to give some help on handmade buttonholes . . . again, providing the material scraps and needles and thread.
- *Alterations Annie* will show a little bit about making garments fit properly. Allowing the ladies to practice fitting an oversized and an undersized garment would provide fun as well as information!
- *Fancy Fanny* will demonstrate more 'advanced needlework.'
- *Cut-a-caper Cathy* will show how to lay out and cut a pattern.

(These will all be more delightful if the sewers and instructors could add to the flavor of the clinic by dressing up to suit their field.)

Be sure to add more workshops or delete those suggested as your local talent and schedules permit.

12. Sew nice:

Make some fabric flowers to match those in the centerpieces. (Instructions for some are found in Chapter 11 of this Resource Manual.)

Let every lady embroider her name on a 3-inch square of material. One will collect them and put them together to make a patchwork quilt or pillow cover for a new mother, a missionary, or someone you love who is leaving the area—or just to give as a marvelous doorprize at the next get-together.

Make patchwork pin cushions out of bits of calico.
Make a gingham dog or a calico cat (see figure 8).

13. Pour a second cup of coffee and read the following story about a patchwork quilt. (After this story is read it would be a grand moment to have those who have brought their own quilts to show them and share their "stories.")

Quilt Patterns

Turkey Tracks—This pattern is in one size only and measures 18″ finished. Usually such a quilt measures 72 x 90 inches.

Churn Dash is an old pattern taken from the design of the paddle in a butter churn. It is made in two sizes, a 15-inch square and a 10-inch square.

Rob Peter to Pay Paul is made of two colors or prints and is a delightful design. Patterns are given for both the 15-inch and 18-inch size blocks. It would look well either with alternating plain blocks or put together with sashwork.

The Greek Cross is done in three colors and/or prints and would look nice either with every block made in the pattern, or with plain blocks or sash-work separating the blocks. I'm partial to having the blocks separated by plain blocks as the design is more outstanding when put together that way.

Pattern is often given in four sizes but most commonly for a 75 x 105-inch quilt or 15-inch blocks.

If you are interested in any other patterns check with your local fabric store or stitchery specialty shop.

Figure 7

Patterns for Gingham Dog and Calico Cat

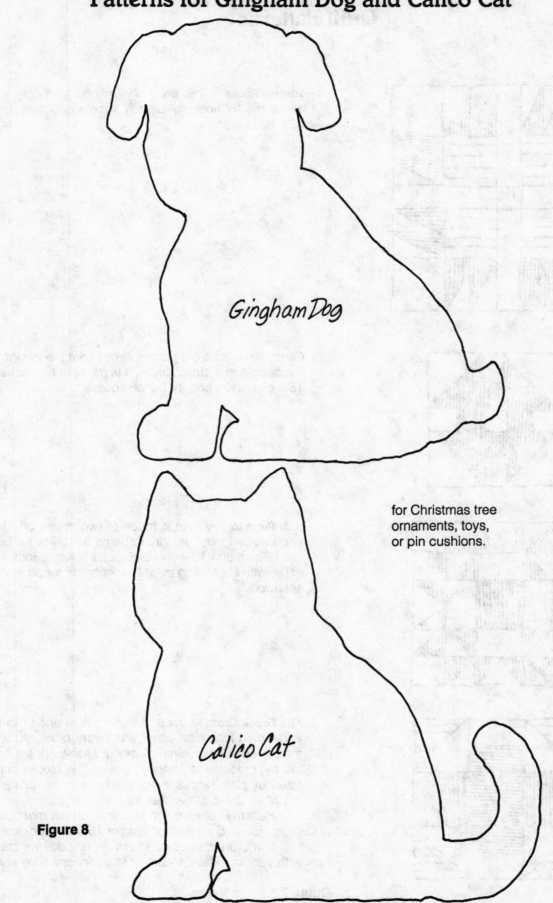

Gingham Dog

for Christmas tree
ornaments, toys,
or pin cushions.

Calico Cat

Figure 8

MEMORIES

When my mother and father moved to Florida, they sent me many family antiques and mementos that have been part of my heritage. One of these antiques is an old clock that was a wedding present to my grandmother and grandfather. I can close my eyes as I hear the sound and recall the sweet memories of my childhood. Another treasure is the little rocking chair whose squeak kept time to my grandmother's songs as she rocked me to the snipping of green beans. Both antiques now have a place of honor in our home, waiting for grandchildren of the future.

In one box, along with a yellowed sun bonnet and monogrammed pillow covers, there was an old quilt folded inside out. I will never forget the reverence I felt as I unfolded this quilt and saw the tiny patches of silk squares and rectangles stitched together with the smallest stitches imaginable. There are satins, brocades, taffetas, files, twills, grosgrains and moire. There is almost every kind of old-fashioned flower represented: bleeding hearts, tiny Scotch thistles, daisies, clover, bachelor's buttons, carnations, a beautiful changeable taffeta rose, lily-of-the-valley, and iris. I know this great-grandmother must have loved flowers as my mother and I do. The colors told me a lot too. A deep red is the predominate color, my favorite color to wear. Every other color is represented also. There are many checks, stripes and plaids, especially of reds and greens. I can imagine the dresses my grandmother and her sisters wore with full skirts dancing and dark curls tossing. There are also patches that must have come from my great-grandfather's ties for I see some dignified grays and navy blues with discreet designs that might have belonged to him.

I have never seen a quilt pattern exactly like this one but it seems to be a variation of the "stripes and squares" pattern. Each piece was sewn on a piece of cotton material on the back to strengthen the silk. Sometimes the stripes were put together as a crazy quilt is fashioned. Other squares were put together as quilt squares are usually made. The cotton backing gave me insight into my great-grandmother's personality too, since different prints as well as plain material scraps were used. These prints were probably used as aprons or house dresses.

The quilt was made by my great-grandmother, Mary Baker Kennedy, wife of Alexander Kennedy, who lived in Johnstown, Pennsylvania. As a child I used to sit at the dinner table for what seemed interminable hours, listening to stories about the branches of our family tree. From these stories I learned that the Alexander Kennedy home was high on a hill in this western Pennsylvania town, and was spared the ravages of the Johnstown flood. Otherwise it would have been lost (as were most of the town's homes) and I probably would not have this beautiful quilt.

Cherishing this quilt has triggered my interest in quilting and has led to my teaching other women to appreciate and make heirlooms for the future.

Betty Shanor Koss lives in Edina, Minnesota. She is married and is the mother of three daughters and three sons.

PATHWORK OF PROMISES

Now end your Patchwork Party with a Patchwork of Promises Bible Study

God does not put our lives together in a crazy-quilt fashion and as the patches of our lives are sewn in place a pattern becomes visible. We can live by faith, knowing that our lives are not haphazardly arranged when the Saviour enters into them.

Let the women take out their Bibles and look first at Philippians 1:6. The Lord Jesus will keep right on working out the pattern begun when our faith was placed in Him, until the day of our meeting Him face to face.

Now have each woman look at Proverbs 31:10-31. Use a version of the Scripture such as Berkeley *or another less familiar translation.*

(1) Notice how many verses refer to the work of her hands.

(2) Notice also that so many of these qualities can be realized at different times in our lives as women.

  • Look back over the pattern of your life and make some notes on a slip of paper where these circumstances have fit. Take some time to share them with one another.

(3) Will you trust Christ to cause you to become that kind of woman?

  • List some of the special qualities you would ask God to work into the pattern of your life, beginning today.

  • Then commit yourself to the cutting and shaping necessary to have Him do His special work in your life.

(4) At each table the women might pick a promise that has been written on a tiny piece of paper (perhaps shaped like a spool of thread) either from Proverbs 31 or from various parts of Scripture. These have been pinned to a large pincushion in the middle of the table. They can be read and each promise shared as to how it could apply to their lives right now.

16
KITCHEN FIXIN'S

1. Have every hostess bring her cutest or cleverest coffee pot filled with daisies and greens and/or other kitchen utensils for a centerpiece.

2. Mimeograph little coffee pot programs (see figure 9) which include favorite recipes collected at a previous meeting.

3. Select several women to prepare these recipes and bring samples to share with the rest of the group. This needs to be done in a ratio of at least 1 to 6—1 dish or loaf to every 6 women—so everyone gets a taste.

4. For a spicy starter disguise ads the women can identify. Cut ads from newspapers or magazines, deleting the product and its name, leaving just the slogans and trademarks. Mount these on construction paper, number them, and hang them around the room in various places. The women can mingle and get acquainted as they move from ad to ad, writing down the names of the products. The one who gets the most correct wins a prize—possibly this week's coupons.

5. Make up a large batch of "Bible Cookies" (see recipe inside figure 9) to serve with coffee at each table while the women fill in the ingredients for this recipe of "Scripture Cake" using their Bibles:

SCRIPTURE CAKE

1 cup of Judges 5:25	(butter)	
1 cup of Exodus 29:2	(flour)	
2 cups of Nahum 3:12	(figs)	
1 cup of Genesis 24:17	(water)	
1 tsp. of Exodus 16:31	(coriander seed)	
2 cups of Jeremiah 6:20	(sweet cane sugar)	
2 cups of 1 Samuel 30:12	(raisins)	
1 cup of Numbers 17:8	(almonds)	
6 Isaiah 10:14	(eggs)	
1 pinch of Leviticus 2:13	(salt)	
3 tsp. of Amos 8:14	(baking powder)	

Season to taste with 1 Kings 10:2. Spices follow Solomon's advice for a good boy in Proverbs 24:13,14. Beat well and bake as fruit cake.

Bible Cookies

1 cup Genesis 18:8 _____
2 cups Psalm 19:10 _____
2 well beaten Job 6:6 _____
3½ cups Exodus 29:2 _____
1 tsp. Luke 13:21 _____
1 tsp. 1 Corinthians 5:6 _____
2 tsp. Exodus 30:23 _____
½ cup sour Joshua 5:6 _____
1 cup broken Genesis 43:11 _____
1 cup seeded 1 Samuel 25:18 _____
1 cup chopped 2 Kings 20:7 _____

Scripture Lesson from My Kitchen:
Detergent—John 3:30
Knife—Hebrews 4:12
Bleach—Psalm 51:7
Salt—Matthew 5:13
Measuring Cups—Luke 6:38
Singing Teakettle—Psalm 16:11

No matter where I serve my guests,
It seems they like my kitchen best.

Figure 9

Lord of pots and pans and things,
Since I've not time to be
A saint by doing lovely things
Or watching late with Thee,
Or dreaming in the dawn light,
Or storming Heaven's gates,
Make me a saint by getting meals
And washing up the plates.

Although I must have Martha's hands,
I have a Mary mind.
And when I black the boots and shoes,
Thy sandals, Lord, I find.
I think of how they trod the earth.
What time I scrub the floor,
Accept this meditation, Lord
I haven't time for more.

—The War Cry

A Prayer for Your Kitchen

Man shall not live by bread alone,
Our Lord and Master said,
But by the Living Word of God,
Our souls must needs be fed.

So as I cook and serve the meals,
I will sincerely pray,
That I shall give, along with food
Some Christlike love today.

Now as I clear the meal away,
And wash the pots and pans,
Dear God, please cleanse my
thoughts and heart,
With thine own loving hands.

Man shall not live by bread alone,
So we do pray, Dear Lord,
Please make us very hungry
For a knowledge of Thy Word.

—N.P. Gordon

6. **For Bible Study:**
Try "The Woman in Her Home" chapter from *The New Me* by Gladys Seashore. Allow each table to spend twenty to thirty minutes.

Or invite a speaker to give a few tips on creative homemaking, from the Word of God.

Don't leave without a number or two from a good old-fashioned home-style kitchen band using kitchen utensils as instruments.

17
GOOD NEWS—
YOU ARE LOVED
(Part 1)

1. Buy a classified ad in your local newspaper to announce this special get-together.

2. Print (some inexpensive offset printer will be a good person for you to get to know) your program like a newspaper front page (note the sample [figure 10]) with headlines reading:
   "GOD LOVES YOU" or "YOU ARE LOVED."

3. Cover the tables with newspapers or photocopy collages of newspaper clippings for place mats.

4. Set up a newsstand in the hallway of your meeting place with the news of the day being announced; and the program "newspaper" being "sold" would get the meeting off to a good start.

5. Take advantage of the newsstand to offer some other literature, including tracts or books from a local bookstore, or Scripture portions from The American Bible Society (P.O. Box 5656, Grand Central Station, New York, NY 10163).

6. A pianist should be playing simple songs such as "Jesus Loves Me."

7. A group of children might sing the song that has been visualized and is available from Child Evangelism Fellowship called "Good News." (This could be a prearranged presentation from the preschool department. The children could even wear homemade newspaper hats to sing their Good News song.)

8. Just for fun, give everyone a piece of newspaper. Ask them to hold it behind their backs and try to tear out a heart shape. The one producing the best heart at each table wins a prize.

9. Now, using your "newspaper" as a guide and in any order you choose, move through your want ads, sporting events, etc. Interrupt the program occasionally for your reporter on the street, who will interview some previously-asked people as to how they became aware of the fact that Jesus loved them—and loves them!

GOOD ✝ NEWS

Publishing by *Life with Spice*—(Date)

In Volume   No.

JESUS LOVES YOU

NEWS BULLETIN
(This can be news of a new baby, pending marriage or any special item of interest to the whole group.)

God showed how much he loved us by sending his only Son into this wicked world to bring to us eternal life through his death. (1 John 4:9)

SPORTS NEWS
(This can be your time of EXERCISES, which might take the form of a bit of competition, as in a Relay around the tables . . . passing a sponge ball or what-have-you.

We know how much God loves us because we have felt his love and because we believe him when he tells us that he loves us dearly.(1 John 4:16)

FOOD EDITOR
(Could share a new recipe in this space.)

EDITORIAL
(A short article written by a pastor or one of your women on the GOOD NEWS OF THE DAY: YOU ARE LOVED.)

COMING EVENTS
(This will be your opportunity for announcements.)

When we love each other God lives in us and his love within us grows ever stronger. (1 John 4:12b)

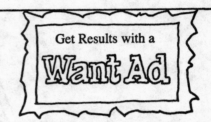

Get Results with a
Want Ad

(Maybe one of your group has something to sell and is advertising anything from a Garage Sale to a Home Party for a product she is selling.)

As we live with Christ, our love grows more perfect and complete. (1 John 4:17)

RECREATION AND TV LISTINGS:

PROGRAM OF "TO TELL THE TRUTH"— See script enclosed.

So you see, our love for him comes as a result of his loving us first. (1 John 4:19)

Figure 10

GOOD NEWS— YOU ARE LOVED
(Part 2)

Your recreation or TV listing can be the following skit, "To Tell the Truth."

To Tell the Truth

Participants:
1 mistress of ceremonies
3 panelists (with their numbers—A,B,C—on small card in front of them on the table
3 women all claiming to be *Charity*
1 woman representing the "sponsor"

Stage:

The mistress of ceremonies will stand (or sit) behind a table or podium on which is a large attractive sign "TO TELL THE TRUTH." The three panelists should sit behind a table at one side of the "stage." The three "Charitys" should sit or stand at the other side of the stage. The three contestants, all claiming to be Charity, should be in some type of costume to add to the appeal of the skit.

M.C.: We welcome you today to TO TELL THE TRUTH. It is good to see you all here in our studio audience. Before we go further, we have a word from our sponsor:

SPONSOR: (Give a two-minute commercial for love, which cannot be purchased anywhere but is available to all who will receive it, in the person of the Lord Jesus. Read from John's love letter, 1 John 4:7-16.)

M.C.: Now we will meet our guests for this program. (Enter three Charitys). Will you please tell us your name?

CHARITY #1: My name is Charity.
CHARITY #2: My name is Charity.
CHARITY #3: My name is Charity.

M.C.: Each of these three ladies claims to be CHARITY. Only one of them is actually CHARITY in whom love lives. Please listen as I read this affidavit that will give you some more information as to her true identity:

"I may not speak every language that the world knows, yet in some way I have been able to communicate in every situation. I am known for my endurance, my humility, and willingness to stand with righteousness. Lots of other things and people will give up, but the hope that I have works under all circumstances."

Now, panel you may begin your questioning. We'll let Mrs. A begin.

MRS. A: Thank you so much. Charity #2, I seem to recall a story I heard about you when your husband came home and announced that you all were going to have to move. Do you remember how you responded?

CHARITY #2: Oh, yes I do! I told him a thing or two! I said that I hadn't worked my fingers to the bone cleaning and painting and shopping to fix this home up for him to come home with an idea like that!

MRS. A: Oh. Charity #3, what was your response? Can you remember?

CHARITY #3:   I remember something that I had read in 1 Peter about wives adapting themselves to their husband's plans, and although I have to admit I was disappointed, because I do love this neighborhood and my friends here, I tried to think of what this move might mean to *him*.

MRS. A: I think I am getting some clues already. But we will see what our first guest has to say. Charity #1, what is your answer?

CHARITY #1:   At first I thought he had lost his job and I began to cry. (Takes out her hanky and sheds a few tears of self-pity.) This kind of thing always happens to me. I just never have any luck—

M.C.:   (Interrupts with a little bell.) We must move along with the questioning. Now to Mrs. B.

MRS. B: Charity, I have known that your reputation in your own neighborhood is a good one. Surely I will be able to discover which of you is the real Charity when I ask this question: How do you react to the many interruptions occurring in the midst of your busy day? How do you respond to your persistent neighbors who always seem to need a favor done, and then, when *you* have a request or a need they cannot find time?

Also, how do you handle it when you discover that you're being talked about in an unkind way at the coffee parties?

Charity #1, what do you say?

CHARITY #1:   I have tried my best but it is never good enough. I have learned that there will always be people like me, apparently just made to be walked on. My husband tells me that I am just too good to people, and that is why they always try to take advantage of me.

MRS. B: You certainly are to be pitied, you poor dear.

Charity #3, what is your answer?

CHARITY #3:   My answer is a simple one. Jesus lives in me, and I found out a long time ago that the Christ in me suffereth long and is kind. Since I am inadequate to cope with even the most mundane problems in my life on my own, I am learning to allow Christ in me to cope. He is even in charge of my time schedule, and since that is the case, the moments of stress are His too!

MRS. B: Your confidence and peace are refreshing. Charity #2, what is your relationship to your problem neighbor?

CHARITY #2:   Well, if I can I just avoid her. Her children are continually running back and forth between our yard and house. I try to keep out of her way by not complaining about the children. I know one thing, I would never ask her to do a thing for me, because that would only lead to obligations that neither of us could fulfill. Anyway, I don't think Jesus meant your next door neighbors when He talked about loving your neighbor. I take care of that in our annual missionary offering where I give to help those who work with the less fortunate—the really needy ones. No needy ones live next door to me!

M.C.:   (Rings bell again.) Thanks so much for that insight. We shall move along now and Mrs. C. will ask her question.

MRS. C: This has certainly been an interesting group of guests. I think I would just like to know how Charity thinks in regards to the present condition of not only our community, but the future of the world in general. Charity #2, let us hear from you on this point.

CHARITY #2: I know I have been doing a lot of talking, but this is one thing I don't even like to think about, much less talk about. I have always figured that things are bad, but they could be a lot worse. If I can just keep my own kids in line, and food on our table, the future can take care of itself. As far as heaven or things like that, I probably won't end up there, but at least I won't be alone wherever I am.

MRS. C: Now, can we have your response, Charity #1?

CHARITY #1: I think that everyone should try to be aware of what everyone else has to say about the future, and even though I am sometimes afraid to hear it, I love my family enough to want to do what I can to know what is going to happen in our future. I try, for example, to never miss the morning horoscope, and although I have to admit I have some moments of confusion, if a new speaker claims some knowledge of the future I try to make arrangements to hear him. This is the least I can do to help solve the problems of the world.

MRS. C: Well, I am not sure if I can agree that that is the best way, but let's hear from Charity #3.

CHARITY #3: The future of our community, with its integration problems, economic problems, welfare and family problems doesn't look too promising, that's for sure. The future of the world has even greater threats. But it really isn't news—because Jesus said that in the world we would have problems, even tribulation and persecution. I just take hope in His promise that He has overcome the world. Christ in me means hope that cannot fail.

M.C.: Our time is up and you have all had the opportunity to decide which you believe is the real CHARITY. We will ask the audience, along with our panel, to vote for number 1, number 2, or number 3.

Tally up the votes and ask the real Charity to please stand up.

(If you have time, you might want to include the introduction of the other charities, to find out their real names and what they really do.—i.e., Charity #1 is really self-pity, masquerading under the name of love. Her energy is consumed in introspection, self-punishment and pity. But this will soon stop because she is thinking about getting into some other line of work! Charity #2 is really self-confidence, masquerading under the name of love through strength of character. Her occupation might be doing good works, but since she is so often laid off she is frustrated. After all, she *is* highly qualified for almost any job!

Involvement ideas:
1. Let each lady become a partner to the one sitting next to her. Let them select a phrase from 1 Corinthians 13 which they can take to heart. Then, on large red hearts or on newspaper hearts, encourage them to use magazine pictures and phrases to illustrate the quality of love defined in the phrase they choose. Have them take these home and tape them to their refrigerator doors as a love reminder! (Let these be shared either by the entire group or by those at their own table. Be sure to set a time limit.)

2. This get-together could be closed with the unison reading of 1 Corinthians 13, replacing the word *love* with *Christ in me . . .*

3. Small group prayer, or around-the-table prayer in small groups is so helpful, particularly after discussing such personal thoughts as Christ-life within. Allow each woman to select a prayer thought from 1 Corinthians 13 and to pray for the one seated next to her.

4. Figure 11 is a pattern for a heart-shaped pincushion for craft time.

Pincushion

For a
puffy pincushion
cut two hearts
from red felt
and letters from
white using the
pattern.

Sew edges together
by hand with
eyelet ruffling
between. Stuff
just before closing
with fibre-fill or
cotton.

Figure 11

18
SUGAR AND SPICE . . .

(And Frogs, Snails & Puppy Dog Tails)

Have a Life with Spice get-together for mothers and their preschool or elementary school age daughters. (A corresponding father and son get-together follows.)

1. Decorate the tables with a good ship lollipop made from construction paper stapled to a Styrofoam block with a paper mast glued to a dowel and stuck in the block. Make faces and hats to put on lollipops. Then stick them in the block to represent the ship's crew.

2. A second option is making a cake house with a frosted roof and candy windows, surrounded by lollipop trees.

3. Sing songs like "A Spoonful of Sugar Helps the Medicine Go Down" from *Mary Poppins* or "Truly Scrumptious" from *Chitty Chitty Bang Bang.*

4. Choose two or three pairs of mothers and daughters to act out fairy tales or nursery rhymes for the others to guess.

5. Make caramel apples together.

6. Read the story of the gingerbread man or present a hand puppet rendition. Distribute pre-baked gingerbread men and decorate with raisins, cinnamon candies and white icing. You may also want to distribute large, round sugar cookies and paint faces using actual paint brushes and thin, colored icing.

7. If space permits, recreate a life-size candyland game to be walked through, perhaps in and out of the church corridors.

8. For refreshments serve sweet goodies like cinnamon rolls, marshmallow clouds, gumdrop animals, peppermint ice cream, chocolate pinwheels, or lemonade.

9. Have a little mother-to-daughter chat using the nursery rhyme—

   There was a little girl with a little curl
   Right in the middle of her forehead.
   When she was good, she was very, very good
   But when she was bad, she was horrid!

10. Have a mother and daughter make faces at one another. "This is how I look when I'm glad—or mad—or afraid." (All of us can make these faces because we really are made of sugar and spice!) Read Romans 7:21-25. Jesus wants to make our lives sweet, and as we let His love grow in our hearts, we become more like Him.

FROGS, SNAILS & PUPPY DOG TAILS

Why not a Life with Spice get-together for fathers and sons?!

1. If little girls are made of sugar and spice aren't little boys made of frogs and snails and puppy dog tails?

2. Decorate the tables with big frogs, frog bean bags (see figure 12) or fishing tackle and green table cloths.

3. After the fathers and sons arrive, play a game to get them all seated. Assign each pair an animal sound to imitate and as they wander through the room making their noise they group together with others making the same sound. When there are ten in the group they may all find their places at a table.

4. Tell fish stories with a prize for the tallest tale.

5. Play leap frog.

6. Have a fish pond.

7. Have the boys bring their pets for a pet show. Blue, red, and green ribbon awards should be given to every contestant.

8. Serve hot dogs, hamburgers, and chocolate ice cream cones.

9. Read a couple of Aesop's Fables and assign noises for characters and sound effects in the story.

10. Invite the characters Huckleberry Finn and Tom Sawyer to share a few of their escapades.

11. Tell the story of David killing the bear.

12. Prepare a Bible study for fathers and sons—using the theme, "How God Has Made Us." Use Psalm 139:13-18,23,24. Encourage them to share in their small groups both praise and prayer for God's handi-work. He knows what we are made of—and it is not really frogs and snails—or puppy dog tails!

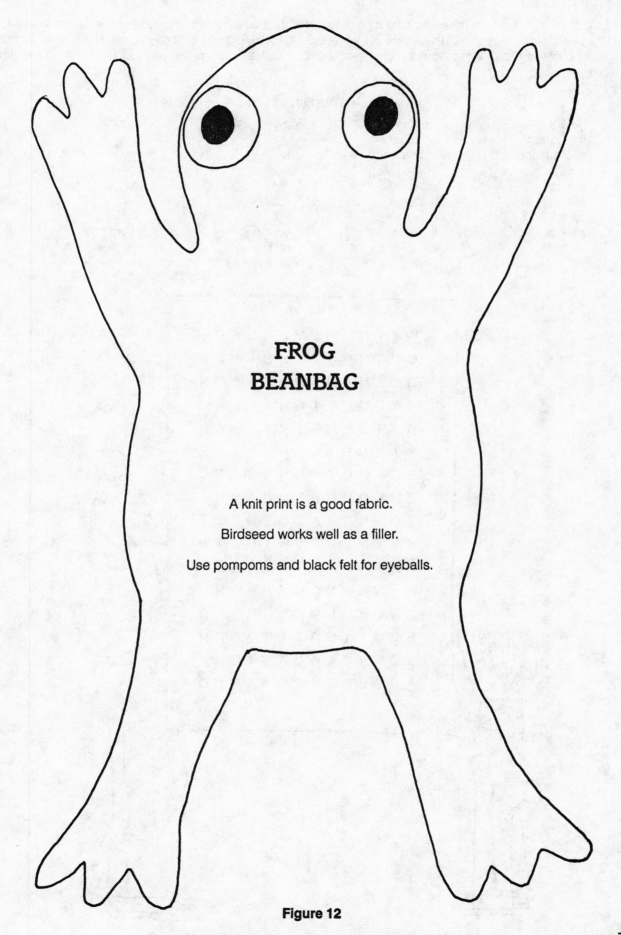

**FROG
BEANBAG**

A knit print is a good fabric.

Birdseed works well as a filler.

Use pompoms and black felt for eyeballs.

Figure 12

13. Distribute this search puzzle and give a prize to the first father and son who complete it. The word list for this search is composed of the words in Matthew 5:14,15,16, exactly as they appear in the King James' Version of the Bible. Words that are grouped together in the word list will be found together in the diagram.

Word List

Ye are	Neither	giveth light	that they
the light	do men	unto	may
of the world.	light a candle,	all	see your
A city	and	that	good
that is	put it	are in	works,
set on	under	the house.	and
an hill	a bushel,	Let	glorify
cannot	but on a	your light	your Father
be hid.	candlestick;	so shine	which is
	and it	before men,	in heaven.

W Y T R X N E M E R O F E B
O H Z H E J T T E O T N U E
R Q I M A H T H A T I S T H
K Y O C D T T G G A L L H I
S D I O H A E I Z I I Q A D
Y T Z N F I L L E G L E T K
Y O Y R H T S H H N N E T C
E S U O H E H T Q S I Y H I
J O M R E Z A E U E E F E T
Y X E Y L C T V W T R I Y S
E A O N A I A I E O A R T E
A U N N I N G G T N R O R L
R N D H O H O H D U N L E D
E L D T I O S Z T N P G D N
E Q U V D L W O A T I D N A
A B U S H E L C S Y A M U C

19
THE FOUR SEASONS

| Fall—Thanksgiving | Spring—Easter |
| Winter—Christmas | Summer—Patriotic |

"Seasonal" Signs of Life with Spice:

Make a door hanging for each season of the year at one of your get-togethers each quarter.

Let everyone who passes by be able to easily identify the homes in the neighborhood where Life with Spicers live! Maybe someone might drop in—imagine that!

For Fall: A grain bundle, straw wreath, or Indian corn with autumn-colored bow.

For Winter: A rafia straw braid with della robbia fruit and large red bow for Christmas.

For Spring: A basket of greens with a bright burlap ribbon bow.

For Summer: A hanging ivy plant—outdoors. Attach a bracket near the front door and hang a simple jute hanger you have macramed at a Life with Spice meeting.

Or make a wreath for all seasons from corn husks (figure 13). The wreath can be made in a variety of ways:

1. Purchase wreaths of straw at a floral supply store. You may complete them by inserting loops of corn-husks

2. You might form the loops and wire them to a coat hanger, being careful to fasten each loop securely and adding the next loop very closely in the ring.

3. Vary the appearance of your wreath by adding a seasonal touch.
   a. For Christmas, spray wreath green and add red bows tucked between the cornhusk loops.
   b. For fall, use bittersweet, pinecones, and nuts, add olive green or gold ribbon tucked between the loops.
   c. For spring, tuck straw flowers into the cornhusks to add color.
   d. For summer, some "permanent" fruit might be attached with wire.

4. Why not add a pretty TAG of oilcloth with the words of Matthew 5:13 and your family name as a front door welcome wreath.

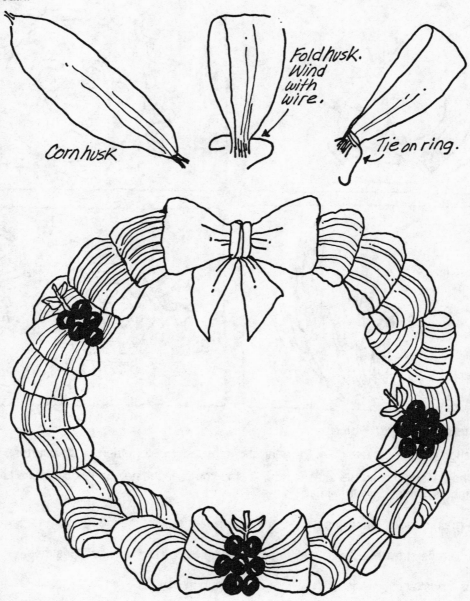

Figure 13

Fall-Thanksgiving

1. Decorate each table with a little harvesttime flavor: autumn leaves, spiced nuts in candy dishes and gingersnaps instead of breads.

2. Make seed picture arrangements on burlap ribbon.

3. Work with bread dough to make a horn of plenty (to be baked, glued onto some rough wood and shellacked).

4. If you like, add fruit made from dough and paint them next meeting.

5. Warm everyone with a cup of spiced tea, and provide the recipe seen below. You might even like to provide the ingredients and baby food jars, which would allow each to make her own sample to take home.

> ## Sweetened Spice Tea
> 2 cups sugar
> ½ cup instant tea
> 1 small jar instant orange breakfast drink.
> 2 pkg. dry lemonade mix
> 1 tsp. cinnamon
> 1 tsp. cloves
> Mix well and store in tightly sealed jar. Use about 2 tsp. per cup. (Some like it with a bit more instant tea added to this recipe.)

6. Have several women bring various kinds of breads: pumpkin bread, nut bread, banana bread, and date bread. Serve with the tea.

7. This is a good time of the year to make seed jars. Not only are they a most attractive reminder of the plenty of our land, but they remind us of the continued miracle of God's goodness in His plan to provide food for our needs.

8. Ask the women to bring an attractive jar (a Mason jar, pickle jar, or apothecary jar will work well). Provide *large* bowls with various sizes and colors of seeds, dried beans or peas. These can be placed on each table or on a central table.

9. Each lady fills her jar by layering the seeds about an inch for each variety of seed. Be sure to begin with the smallest, paying attention to the colors for interest and attractiveness. The larger pumpkin seeds or sunflower seeds should be at the top. (We were able to purchase last year's seeds at a local farm store very inexpensively.) After the top is securely in place (making certain again that the jar is filled to capacity to keep seeds from mixing) tie a checked bow around the neck. You might attach a label with a verse of Scripture. (See figure 14.)

10. Ask some women ahead of time to bring articles from their own homes which represent a particular area of life in which we should give thanks to God. One of these ladies should be seated at each table and be prepared to give a short meditation on that particular theme; i.e., some of her family pictures would suggest thanks to God for family blessings, children, a husband or parents; a Bible might suggest heartfelt gratitude to God for the opportunity of worship and learning to walk closely with Christ without persecution; a globe might suggest gratitude for those who have left our land to serve the Lord in other countries. Allow time for sharing expressions of gratitude—especially for one another gathered around the tables. Then have a time of prayer.

11. As a meaningful closing, a song of praise or thanksgiving might be sung by the entire group or a soloist. Then have one representative from each table offer a sentence prayer before the benediction.

 UNLESS YOU ARE BORN AGAIN YOU CAN NEVER GET INTO THE KINGDOM OF GOD... JOHN 3:3

GOD IS LOVE AND ANYONE WHO LIVES IN LOVE IS LIVING WITH GOD AND GOD IS LIVING IN HIM. 1 JOHN 4:16

 FOR GOD SO LOVED THE WORLD HE GAVE HIS ONLY SON. JOHN 3:16

ALL BELIEVERS WERE OF ONE HEART AND MIND AND NO ONE FELT WHAT HE OWNED WAS HIS OWN; EVERYONE WAS SHARING. ACTS 4:32

I HAVE BEEN CRUCIFIED WITH CHRIST AND I MYSELF NO LONGER LIVES... BUT CHRIST LIVES IN ME... Galatians 2:20

THINK ABOUT THINGS THAT ARE PURE AND LOVELY AND DWELL ON THESE FINE GOOD THINGS IN OTHERS. PHILIPPIANS 4:8

JESUS TOLD THEM, I AM THE TRUTH, THE WAY AND THE LIFE...NO ONE CAN GET TO THE FATHER EXCEPT BY MEANS OF ME... JOHN 14:6

AND BE SURE OF THIS THAT MATT. 28:20 I AM WITH YOU ALWAYS... EVEN TILL THE END OF THE EARTH.

MAY YOUR ROOTS GO DOWN DEEP INTO THE SOIL OF GOD'S MARVELOUS LOVE. EPHESIANS 3:17

LOVE ONE ANOTHER. I JOHN 2:8

YOU CAN GET ANYTHING YOU ASK FOR IN PRAYER IF YOU BELIEVE. MATTHEW 21:22

ROMANS 10:8 FOR SALVATION COMES FROM TRUSTING CHRIST.

Figure 14

Celebrate Christmas with a birthday party for Jesus. Mimeograph programs that resemble birthday cards.

The following is an account of a successful Christmas Life with Spice gathering:

"We met first in the church sanctuary where a short musical concert—presented by a Christian high school band—soon helped everyone to begin to enjoy the holiday atmosphere.

"The name tags were shaped to represent the twelve months of the year, and the women were to pick up their appropriate birthday tag. Confusion resulted! So, we simply allowed everyone a tag regardless of her birthdate. We wanted the group to mingle and we succeeded!

"*A Holly Walk* was planned. The women had assembled a wonderful array of homecrafted items that everyone wanted to enjoy. By using large construction-paper holly leaves a route was planned in and out of the various rooms in the church where the articles were displayed. The route led past the church kitchen where brunch plates of food were picked up and carried into the larger room where the eating and the program were to take place.

"Each table was decorated for a special month. We had made Swedish Christmas trees at a previous Life with Spice gathering (see figure 15) and it was simple to adapt each to fit the various months. We used maybaskets of tiny flowers for May, tiny felt hearts for February, flags and firecrackers for July, sailboats from walnut shells for August, etc. (See figure 16.) (There was one woman responsible for each table.)

"Prizes were given out periodically throughout the get-together—one for those whose birthday was in January-February-March, another to be competed for by those born in April-May-June, etc.

"This was a great day to celebrate Christ's coming to the world, and also to share in the celebration of our re-birthdays. Several women were prepared to witness to their 'second birthday' and to their first Christmas spent in Christ. This was an unforgettable part of this special Life with Spice."

"Then, one of our young mothers gave a few tips on how to more effectively celebrate Christmas with one's family.

"*Candles* at each place (birthday candles were placed in marshmallows and then on tiny paper doilies) were lit by the women as a guest sang, "The Birthday of a King."

Some verses from Exodus *(The Living Bible)* are favorites of mine in celebration: *"And in the future, when your children ask you, 'What is this all about?' you shall tell them . . . this celebration shall identify you as God's people, just as much as if his brand of ownership were placed upon your foreheads"* (Exod. 13:14,16).

One room had been set aside for a toy and gift shop. It was well-stocked with secondhand or next-to-new children's clothes and toys. Everything sold for 25¢ and helped several of us whose Christmas gift list was long! The proceeds were put in the nursery fund.

Make a Christmas banner:
Cut an 18 x 8-inch rectangle of green felt and glue the top edge over a 9-inch dowel stick. Tie green yarn at each end to hang. Cut large letters from red felt spelling *NOEL* and glue vertically along left side of banner. From silver or gold foil cut a small square, a star, a skyline of Bethlehem, an angel, and baby Jesus in the manger (see figure 17).
Print copies of the verses to glue on these shapes. Have the ladies bring 25 pieces of red-and-white-striped peppermint candy or any other kind of their choice to tie on banner. Thread a large needle with yarn and pull through the felt to backside, then to front again and cut, leaving two long strands. Tie the strands around one end of candy where the cellophane is twisted. One sweet each day from December 1 to 24 is a special treat and day counter.

The Scripture Christmas Tree:

Are You Interested in sharing the Scriptures with others?

The Christmas season especially reminds us that our Lord loved us enough to become one of us, to sacrifice Himself for us so that we may understand once and for all that God *is,* and always *was,* and *always will be;* that God is love. Love is the greatest power there is, and love is the meaning of Christmas. Christmas is love in action.

What is one way in which you can put your love into action at Christmas?

One way is to give others the Word which so beautifully expresses this love. Decorating a tree at Christmas time has been a custom observed for centuries. Decorating a tree with the Scriptures is a comparatively new idea, especially since its purpose is to be *untrimmed.*

How does one decorate a Scripture tree?

The American Bible Society has several items which are useful and attractive as "ornaments." Small portions of the New Testament books and special Christmas selections with strings or ribbons attached for hanging on the tree are simple to prepare, inexpensive to purchase, and give a festive appearance.

Where does one place a Scripture tree?

Since the purpose of the tree is to reach others with the Word, it should be placed where people pass by. Trees of this kind have been placed in a variety of public places—supermarkets, hospital lounges, shopping centers, lobbies of banks, institutions, and on the sidewalk in busy areas.

Is the tree only an ornament?

Someone should be stationed near the tree to invite those passing by to stop and select a piece of Scripture from the tree—*to untrim the tree.* These are given as gifts, not to be sold. As materials are taken from the tree they should be replaced so that it is always fully decorated.

This project was first carried out in December 1968, in conjunction with a women's Bible Class in Harlem, New York. On a Saturday afternoon, three weeks before Christmas, a tree was so decorated and placed on the sidewalk in front of the church where the group met. In two hours, 300 pieces of Scripture were distributed. The idea has spread to all parts of the country and is a project for all ages, proving to be an excellent way of witnessing and placing the Word in the hands of many.

Your best resource for ideas for material to put on the tree is the American Bible Society catalog: A HANDBOOK FOR ABS VOLUNTEERS, American Bible Society, P.O. Box 5656, Grand Central Station, New York, NY 10163.

Make a Birthday Cake for Jesus:

An angel-topped cake symbolic of the Christmas story can become a lovely and tasty holiday tradition at your home. The Christmas cake is made with a set of four tier cake pans. These can be either the 10", 8", 6", and 4" sizes, or the smaller 9", 7" 5" and 3" ones.

If you are using the larger pans, mix up a triple batch of your favorite spice cake recipe, or three packages of spice cake mix. (A double batch or two packages will be enough batter for the smaller pans.) If you have any cake batter left over, make a few cupcakes.

Bake the cake layers—cool in pans for 10 minutes, then cool on racks. Cut the smallest layer into a star shape. (Hint: line the pan bottoms with greased circles cut from brown paper or with wax paper.)

Next make *snowdrift icing.* Bring 1½ cups light corn syrup to a boil. Beat two egg whites to soft peaks and add ⅛ tsp. salt. Pour the hot syrup slowly on the egg whites, beating constantly until peaks form when beaters are lifted. Then stir in 1 tsp. vanilla. Spread the bottom cake layer with icing, building to the star-shaped layer. On this layer place a small, purchased angel figurine, or make your own.

The angel symbolizes the heavenly throng who sang "Peace on earth," and the star represents the star in the East which guided the shepherds and the Magi to the manger.

Then place 20 red birthday candles (red is the color of love and joy) around the bottom tier to represent the centuries elapsed since the first Christmas.

Trim the edge of each tier with gold dragées and place the cake on a gold paper doily. The spice flavor of the cake represents the frankincense, the dragées represent the myrrh, and the doilies represent the gold—the gifts of the Magi to the Christ child.

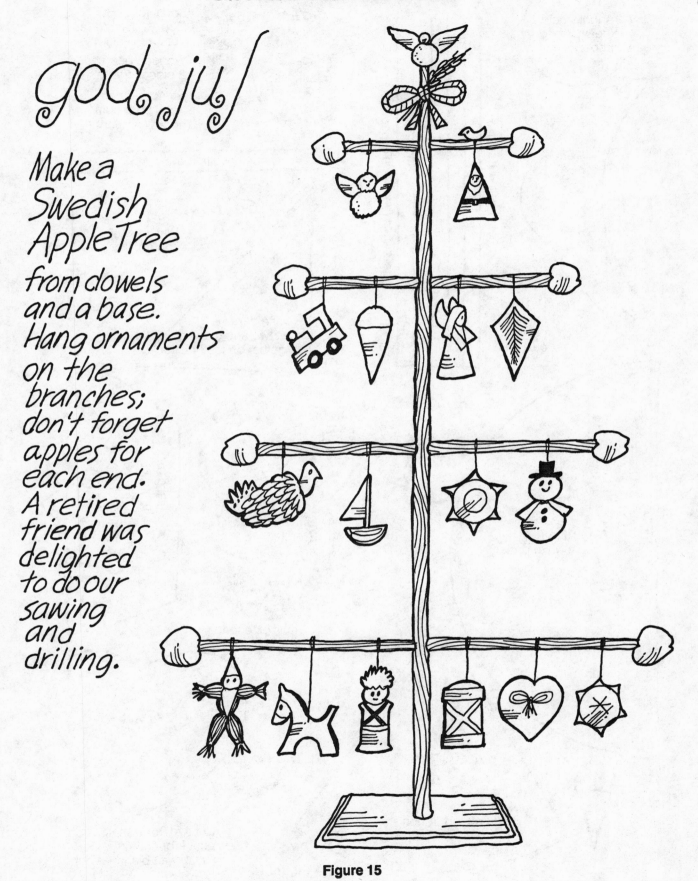

god jul

Make a Swedish Apple Tree from dowels and a base. Hang ornaments on the branches; don't forget apples for each end. A retired friend was delighted to do our sawing and drilling.

Figure 15

Table Decorations

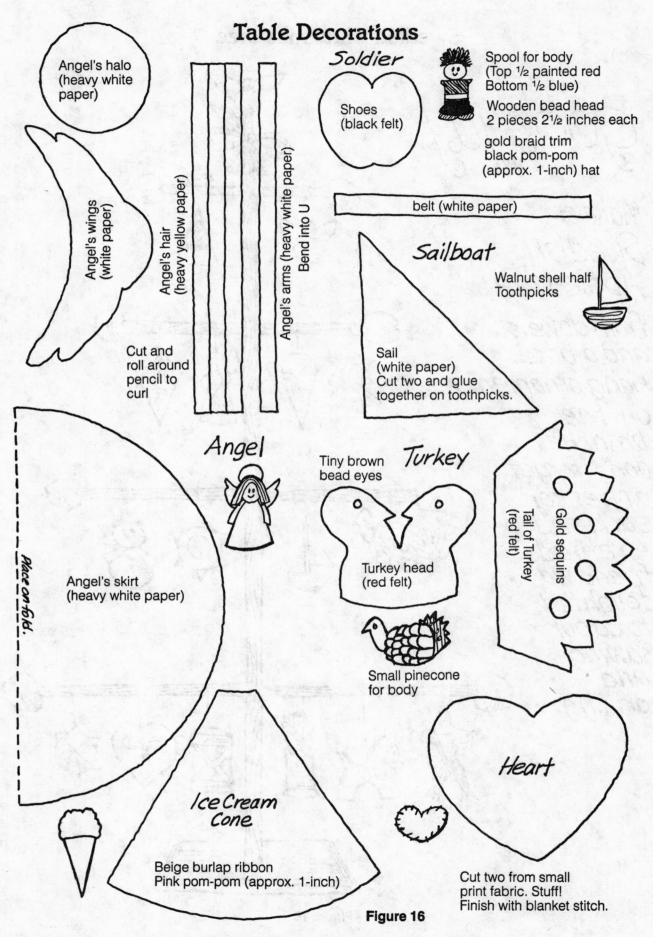

Angel's halo (heavy white paper)

Soldier

Shoes (black felt)

Spool for body (Top ½ painted red Bottom ½ blue)

Wooden bead head 2 pieces 2½ inches each

gold braid trim black pom-pom (approx. 1-inch) hat

belt (white paper)

Angel's wings (white paper)

Angel's hair (heavy yellow paper)

Angel's arms (heavy white paper) Bend into U

Cut and roll around pencil to curl

Sailboat

Walnut shell half Toothpicks

Sail (white paper) Cut two and glue together on toothpicks.

Angel

Tiny brown bead eyes

Turkey

Place on fold.

Angel's skirt (heavy white paper)

Turkey head (red felt)

Tail of Turkey (red felt)

Gold sequins

Small pinecone for body

Heart

Ice Cream Cone

Beige burlap ribbon Pink pom-pom (approx. 1-inch)

Cut two from small print fabric. Stuff! Finish with blanket stitch.

Figure 16

Christmas Banner

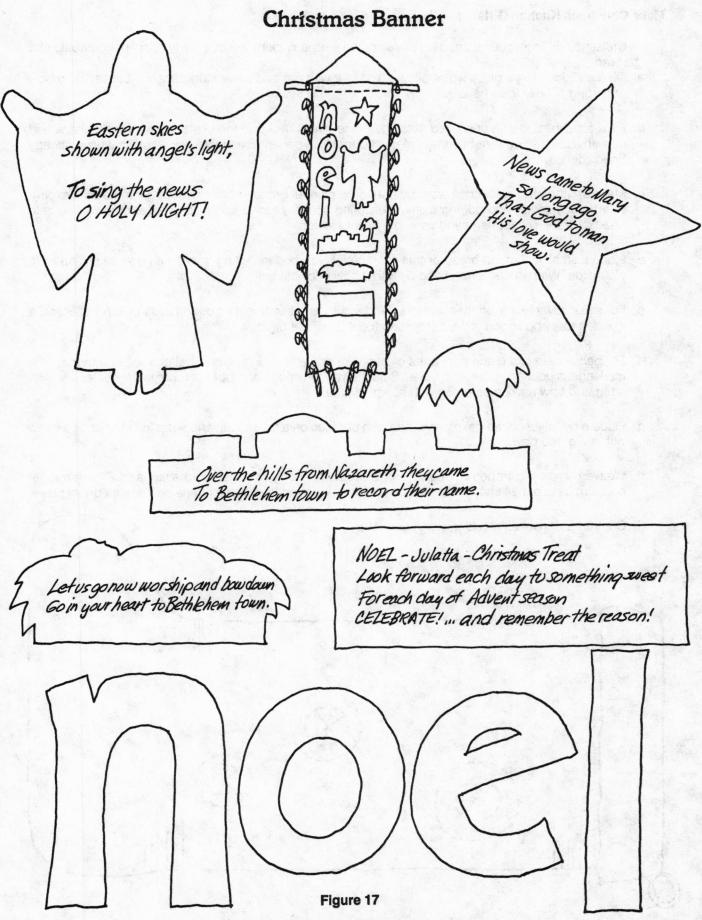

Eastern skies shown with angel's light,

To sing the news O HOLY NIGHT!

News came to Mary so long ago, That God to man His love would show.

Over the hills from Nazareth they came To Bethlehem town to record their name.

Let us go now worship and bow down Go in your heart to Bethlehem town.

NOEL - Julatia - Christmas Treat Look forward each day to something sweet For each day of Advent season CELEBRATE! ... and remember the reason!

Figure 17

Make Christmas Kitchen Gifts:

A Christmas gift from your kitchen to take along on a holiday call, give as a party prize, or contribute to a bazaar:

a. Take a simple, large glass water pitcher and fill it with red and white striped candy canes. Tie a bow and sprig of holly to its handle.

b. Fill a small basket with unshelled nuts and place a nut cracker in the center. Wrap in cellophane tied up with a big, red bow; or fill a glass meat chopper with pecans, cashews, or walnuts that have already been shelled.

c. Make an attractive bath accessory by pouring a colorful granular laundry detergent into an inexpensive brandy snifter and adding a little measuring scoop, or try a water conditioner or jewel-like bath beads. Wrap in cellophane and tie with a bow to match.

d. Place a small loaf of nut bread or fruit cake on a little wooden cutting board with a small slicing knife alongside. Wrap in cellophane and tie with a bow and little bells.

e. For salad lovers fill a bright-colored colander with an assortment of dried herbs or spices. Stand a wooden fork and spoon in the center tied together with a big bow.

f. For pancake lovers place packages of pancake or waffle mix in a useful pitcher-bowl with measure markings, a pouring spout, and cover. Stand a wooden spoon or rubber scraper in the center tied with a big, red bow and ornamented with sprigs of pine.

g. Place a beautiful coffee cake decorated with cherries on a lazy susan and wrap in cellophane tied up with a big, red bow.

h. Weave narrow red ribbon through the openwork of a berry or vegetable basket and fill with midget popcorn balls or ball-shaped Christmas cookies. Wrap in colored cellophane and tie with bright bows.

i. Crochet a Christmas stocking (see figure 18).

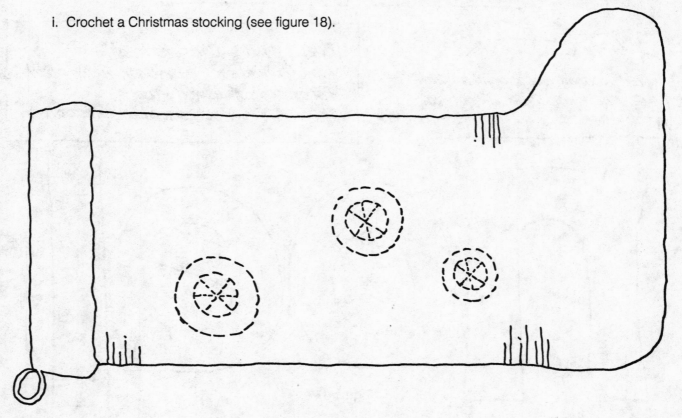

Christmas Stocking

ch—chain; sc—single crochet; dc—double crochet; dec—decrease; sl—slip; hdc—half double crochet; dtr—double treble.

Materials:
worsted weight yarn—5 oz. of red and 1½ oz. of white
yarn needle
crochet hook size "E"

Gauge:
4 dc = 1 inch
stocking will measure 18 inches from top to heel

Make two
ch 33, sc in second ch from hook and in each to end. ch 2, turn.
row 1: sc
row 2: dc, dec 1 dc each side.
row 3: sc
row 4: dc
row 5: sc
row 6: dc, dec 1 at each side.
repeat last 4 rows.
work in pattern of 1 sc row, 1 dc row even for 27 rows, ending with a sc row completed.
row 7: dc across and ch 22.
row 8: sc in second ch from hook and each to end, sc in each sc.
for other side, do ch row on this row, so you can have same side outside on completed stocking.
work 17 more rows in pattern. end. side with dc row appearing to stand out is right side.
sew using backstitch, right sides together, rounding off corners on heel and toe. Steam press lightly on low.

Cuff
ch 64, dc in third ch from hook and each remaining chain to end, ch 2, turn.
work 2 more rows even.
scallop
sl st in first st, * sc in first dc, hdc in second dc in third dc, tr in fourth dc, 5 d tr in fifth dc, tr in sixth dc, dc in seventh dc, hdc in eighth dc, sc in ninth dc, sl st in tenth dc. Repeat from * to end.

Sew cuff on: ch 30 and work 1 row sc for hanger.

Large snowflake
make one for each side.
ch 5, form in ring.
ch 4 * ch 1, d tr in ring, repeat from * 13 more times.
sl st into top of ch.
sc in one ch between d tr, ch 2, sc in same ch, ch 1, repeat around. end.

Medium flake
make same as large, but make tr instead of d tr, and make 12 (counting first ch) instead of 15

Small flake
make the same, but with dc, and 9 dc in ring.
sew snowflakes to stocking with large at top, medium in middle, and small at bottom.

Figure 18

The week before the *egg*citing Easter gathering have the women select various jobs by drawing, from an Easter basket, egg-shaped pieces of paper with jobs written out. For instance, you'll need a dozen women to *eggs*ibit hats, another dozen *eggs*pert hostesses to pour coffee and make the guests welcome, four d*egg*orators to assemble materials for the sparkle-dust Easter eggs, and a dozen women to express why they believe in the Resurrection.

1. Decorate your tables with Easter baskets filled with cellophane grass and enough Styrofoam eggs for each person. Tie a gingham or calico ribbon—cut with a pinking shears—in a big bow on the handle. Cover tables with pastel-colored sheets or paper tablecloths to match the bow. This will make your tables look *eggs*ilarating!

2. Have the hostess at each table count the number of eggs the women cooked that morning for breakfast as she introduces them to one another. The table with the largest number of eggs cooked wins a basketful of chocolate eggs for a delightful *eggs*perience!

3. Then unscramble a few eggs. Beforehand, mimeograph a list of different ways of cooking eggs with the letters scrambled. For instance: benedict, soft-cooked, hard-boiled, poached, soufflé, omelette, deviled, sunny-side-up. The woman who unscrambles them the fastest and most correctly wins the prize—a dozen eggs!

4. Do the word search, "Names for Christ," together at the tables (see figure 19).

5. This is an *egg*specially good time for an Easter hat parade emphasizing the theme, "Life with Spice." Select women to bring hats decorated with articles from the kitchen and then *egg*sibit them in a parade around the room accompanied by the song "Easter Parade."

6. Here are instructions for d*egg*orating the Styrofoam eggs at the tables using paper napkins.

Materials:
Styrofoam eggs
paper napkins—3-ply with Easter design
paint brushes
white glue thinned a little with water
saucer of diamond dust (available through any craft store)

Directions:
Tear out part of the Easter design on the napkin. Separate the top ply on which it is printed. Paint the Styrofoam egg with the thinned glue. Pat design from napkin into place. Allow to dry a minute or two.

Cover egg with as many designs as desirable.

Paint the entire egg with the glue mixture. Roll the egg in a saucer of diamond dust or sprinkle it from a shaker. Shake off excess into saucer. Allow to dry for a few minutes.

Try making them in various sizes utilizing several parts of the design in the napkin. They make lovely place-card holders or centerpieces.

7. Sing an Easter song either as a group or special musical number to introduce a brief ten-minute message from Scripture. Tell the Easter story simply but thoroughly, emphasizing the verses Romans 10:9 and 10 in particular. Close with women sharing their testimonies of why they believe in the Resurrection.

Word Search

NAMES FOR CHRIST

```
O D Y G E F I L F O D A E R B Z P R L
Z B O W S R I T I K R O N R E V O G E
R D X V T F Q P E G J D C B T T U B U
L E A D E R U M L H H F J E S U S M N
K L G N H C N A R B P T N A E W R A A
E I I N Z E P W R A X O V Y I B L L M
T V N V E A N E M W T I R T R Z A M M
A E P G M S T E M S O S N P P Y W I I
C R C W B R S E R U Z E G X H B G G K
O E O N O S D E R A S H W N G U I H A
V R B F I I N Z M S Z O T R I Q V T G
D C M A A R B A F J F A S U H N E Y E
A O H T O F P G M H K O N L R M R P M
C B O C A H P L A E C H R I S T N O O
F R K R O T A E R C S H E P H E R D M
```

—from *The War Cry*

INSTRUCTIONS: The hidden words listed to the right appear in
the puzzle, forward, backward, up, down and diagonally. Find
each word and put a box around it as shown in the example.

```
O D Y G E F I L F O D A E R B Z P R L
Z B O W S R I T I K R O N R E V O G E
R D X V T F Q P E G J D C B T T U B U
L E A D E R U M L H H F J E S U S M N
K L G N H C N A R B P T N A E W R A A
E I I N Z E P W R A X O V Y I B L L M
T V N V E A N E M W T I R T R Z A M M
A E P G M S T E M S O S N P P Y W I I
C R C W B R S E R U Z E G X H B G G K
O E O N O S D E R A S H W N G U I H A
V R B F I I N Z M S Z O T R I Q V T G
D C M A A R B A F J F A S U H N E Y E
A O H T O F P G M H K O N L R M R P M
C B O C A H P L A E C H R I S T N O O
F R K R O T A E R C S H E P H E R D M
```

Advocate
Almighty
Branch
Corner-Stone
Deliverer
God
High Priest
Jesus
Lamb
Leader
Light
Master
Messenger
Messiah
Morning Star
Nazarene
Prince
Prophet
Rock
Shepherd
Truth
Vine
Witness
Word

Figure 19

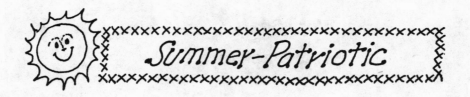
1. Invite the entire family to a special patriotic celebration during the summer! Use your imagination to make the room resplendent in red, white, and blue. Decorate a special area for a stage.

2. Frame or mount presidential portraits available at bookstores, school supply stores, or your public library, and hang them in a picture gallery for the families to tour and identify.

3. As an icebreaker, have families get together and answer "To Tell the Truth", "What's My Name", and "Special Greeting" (see figure 20). Give a prize to the family with the most correct answers.

4. Supply construction paper, costumes, and props and allow fifteen minutes for families to prepare skits reenacting given historical events to present on the stage. Put the scripts in envelopes to be secretly selected.

5. Enjoy a piece of Abe Lincoln's favorite cake (see figure 21) or a George Washington cherry tart with a cup of coffee.

6. A responsive reading of Scripture taken from presidential inaugural addresses (figure 22) and a short message on 2 Chronicles 7:14 might follow. Around each table share ways in which families might more effectively obey this special challenge from God. Close with a rousing chorus of "America" (verse 4):

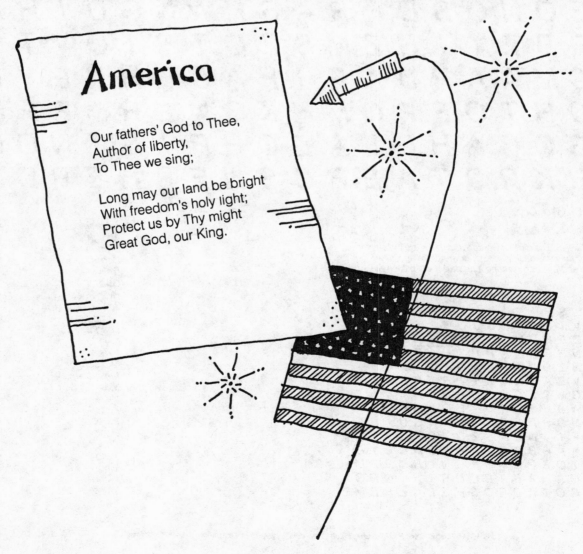

America

Our fathers' God to Thee,
Author of liberty,
To Thee we sing;

Long may our land be bright
With freedom's holy light;
Protect us by Thy might
Great God, our King.

To Tell the Truth

True or False

1. Hoover was an orphan at ten, a millionaire at 40.   _____
2. Teddy Roosevelt was the largest President.   _____
3. Taft's approximate weight was 300 lbs.   _____
4. John Adams was the smallest.   _____
5. Woodrow Wilson issued the Emancipation Proclamation.   _____
6. Grover Cleveland was the only president who ever—   _____
   a. Had a man hanged   _____
   b. Was re-elected after leaving the White House.   _____
7. Three Presidents assassinated while in office were Lincoln, Garfield and McKinley.   _____
8. Franklin Roosevelt was born in a mansion.   _____

Answers to *To Tell the Truth* : 1-T, 2-F, 3-T, 4-F (Madison), 5-F (Lincoln), 6-T and T, 7-T, 8-T.

What's My Name?

1. I could lick almost any man in a test of strength.
   I didn't go around looking for trouble.
   People seemed to love my funny stories.
   I am surprised that the short speech I once made is said to be one of the finest expressions found in the English language.
   I was grieved by the Civil War. I was the 16th President, but was killed by an assassin's bullet.

   _____

2. Life was a very serious matter to me.
   It was hard for me to relax. I lost both of my children while they were quite young. My wife was an invalid for most of her life. The Spanish American War was during my administration.
   I was the third President to be killed in office.
   I was the 25th President of the U.S.

   _____

3. The Parcel Post Act was passed during my administration.
   In 1921, I was appointed Chief Justice. We had the first automobile in the White House. I was said to be a jolly soul, but probably should have gone to Weight Watchers.
   I was the 27th President of the United States.

   _____

4. My nickname was "Old Hickory." I was popular among the common people. I fired 2000 federal job holders and gave the jobs to my friends. I was the 7th President.

   _____

5. My nickname was "Old Tippecanoe."
   I was an Indian Fighter. My political campaigns were the most exciting that had ever been held. My grandson became the 23rd President of the U.S.
   I died one month after I became President, so you don't know what kind of President I would have made.

   _____

Answers to WHAT'S MY NAME?: Abraham Lincoln, William McKinley, William Taft, Andrew Jackson, William H. Harrison

Figure 20

Special Greeting

Fill in the blanks. Note the first letter of each answer, and give your country a Special Greeting!

_____ My wife Bess often accompanied my daily constitutionals.
_____ Roaming this land I planted trees, John's my name, if you please.
_____ The Keystone State
_____ Where the Liberty Bell still rings
_____ Still on schedule, here OLD FAITHFUL gives a show
_____ A frank statesman, author and kiteflyer I was.
_____ Original Americans
_____ Lady who took this nation from FLAGS TO STITCHES
_____ A polluting party
_____ Longfellow's here
_____ River where Washington proved he could make a dollar go a long way
_____ Remember! The _____
_____ An All-American Bear
_____ Our first real Moon Man
_____ Ole' Man River
_____ FDR's first lady
_____ American Cowboy Contest
_____ An American songwriter, Berlin
_____ The Golden State
_____ A sea from a Shining Sea

Answers to the SPECIAL GREETING: Harry Truman; Johnny Appleseed; Pennsylvania; Philadelphia; Yellowstone National Park; Ben Franklin; Indians; Betsy Ross; Tea Party; Hiawatha; Delaware; Alamo; Yogi; Astronauts; Mississippi; Eleanor; rodeo; Irving Berlin; California; Atlantic

Figure 20

Abe Lincoln's Favorite Cake

1 cup butter
2 cups sugar
3 cups flour (cake or pastry)
2 tsp. baking powder
1 tsp. vanilla
⅔ cup milk
1 cup chopped blanched almonds
¼ tsp. salt
6 egg whites

Preheat oven to 350°
Cream butter and sugar slightly.
Sift flour and baking powder together and add alternately with milk (to the first mixture).
Add well-floured nuts, then vanilla.
Fold in stiffly-beaten whites of egg, to which salt has been added.
Bake in three layers (8- or 9-inch pans).
Ice with boiled icing, to which add ½ cup candied pineapple and cherries, chopped fine.

Mary Todd made this cake for Lincoln before their marriage, and he declared it "the best in Kentucky."

Figure 21

When Dwight D. Eisenhower was inaugurated, he had George Washington's Bible opened to Psalm 127:1, as well as his own Bible opened to 2 Chronicles 7:14. It is not generally known that ever since Washington's Inauguration, it has been the practice for each president to choose a text to be used at his inauguration.

It was not until President Grant's first term that an official record was kept of the passages used.

The following texts are those chosen by some of our Presidents:

Responsive Reading:

LEADER: ABRAHAM LINCOLN And I heard another out of the Altar say, even so Lord God Almighty, true and righteous are thy judgments. Revelation 16:7. Judge not, that ye be not judged. Matthew 7:1

RESPONSE: THEODORE ROOSEVELT Be ye doers of the word, and not hearers only, deceiving your own selves. James 1:22

LEADER: HERBERT HOOVER Where there is no vision, the people perish: but he that keepeth the law, happy is he. Proverbs 29:18

RESPONSE: FRANKLIN D. ROOSEVELT And now abideth faith, hope, charity, these three; but the greatest of these is charity. 1 Corinthians 13:13

LEADER: JOHN F. KENNEDY Is not this the fast that I have chosen? to loose the bands of wickedness, to undo the heavy burdens, and to let the oppressed go free, and that ye break every yoke? Isaiah 58:6

RESPONSE: DWIGHT D. EISENHOWER If my people, which are called by my name, shall humble themselves, and pray, and seek my face, and turn from their wicked ways; then will I hear from heaven, and will forgive their sin, and will heal their land. 2 Chronicles 7:14

LEADER: HARRY S. TRUMAN Blessed are the peacemakers: for they shall be called the children of God. Matthew 5:9

UNISON: The king's heart is in the hand of the Lord, as the rivers of water: he turneth it whithersoever he will. Proverbs 21:1

Figure 22

Part IV: LEADER'S GUIDE

20
BE IT EVER SO HUMBLE

Be sure to examine all the parts before crossing the threshold with your group. Choose the items best suited to your church group or neighborhood situation—and *actively create your own special event*.

Here is Your Name Tag.
Photocopy and color it. Then staple a bit of grosgrain ribbon to the top, so that it will last longer, and can be used throughout this study.

One
Home in a Garden

1. Using this lesson as a basis for creative get-togethers around the Word of God, think about using baskets of apples for centerpieces, and snacks.

2. Invite a gardener to share some tips on gardening.

3. Have several make the apple cake recipe and bring to the get-together for samples.

4. Invite the women to share memories of their first home.

5. Have you ever tried to see if you could peel an apple completely without breaking the peeling? Try it, and give a prize of gardening gloves, or peeler, or? . . .

Two
Home in a Boat

1. Feature a different color of the rainbow at each table.

2. Share Scripture promises among participants.

3. How about Animal Crackers or rainbow Jello salad for refreshments?

4. Spotlight tips on safe boating practices.

Three
Home in a Mobile Home

1. Offer a prize to the person who has moved the most number of times; to the one who has lived in the most states; and then to the one who bore a child at the most advanced age!

2. Sing, or invite a guest to sing, "Surely Goodness and Mercy Shall Follow Me" . . . "—a Pilgrim was I and a-wandring . . . . "

3. Have available some books or other helps on how to have an effective family altar. A local Christian bookstore might allow you to sell them on consignment.

4. *Moving companies* have available kits on how to make your move—painlessly. Call one or two and perhaps they can offer some favors for the occasion. (We found some Where Are You? map-quiz place mats.)

Four
Home in a Tent

1. Invite the women to bring snapshots or slides of tenting they have enjoyed as a family and share them. Create a mixer game by allowing them to guess the persons in the photos.

2. Special prizes given to mothers of twins.

3. Make up a true or false quiz, either about the Bible story, local facts, or a fun series of situations about the people present.

4. Give a first-aid demonstration about how to handle accidents while camping.

5. "To Tell the Truth" television game is an excellent tool for conveying the truth. Either write your own situations, or refer to the skit "To Tell the Truth" in the chapter "Good News—You Are Loved, Part 2."

Five
Home in a Palace

1. Fun at Farro's—An Egyptian version of an ice cream party. Let everyone make her own sundae! (Instead of a Pike's Peak—enter with a Pyramid for the honored guests.)

2. Babies and creative mothering can be the theme for this get-together, having baskets with babies cuddled inside for centerpieces.

3. This would be a great occasion to have a baby shower for someone in the group, or the assembling of a layette to be sent to a missionary or mission.

4. As the women enter, "Rock-A-Bye-Baby" might be the background music with a mother in a rocker reading to her baby as the focus for a few minutes of devotion.

5. "Palace Living" and "Royal Education" could be an alternate emphasis. Use books, brainteasers, and school days to enhance the Bible study.

6. This could be a day to honor nursery workers and the teachers of children. Use your imagination to affirm their service to the Lord and your recognition of that special ministry.

Six
Home in a Penthouse

1. Ask several women to decorate the tables with some of their own pretty dishes, tablecloth, napkins, centerpieces, etc.

2. Have someone give some tips on setting a pretty table or arranging flowers.

3. Ask one or two people to read (ahead of time!) Karen Mains' *Open Heart—Open Home*, and share some additional ideas of their own.

4. *Think about this!* Arrange for lunch to be served in various homes within your group, and then to meet in a central place for dessert and Bible study.

5. Award guest towels or napkins to those women who have had the most invited—then uninvited—guests in their home recently.

Seven
Home in Army Quarters

1. Ask women ahead of time to be prepared to demonstrate their favorite household hint.

2. Play a game of "The Price Is Right" with household cleaning products. Several articles can be placed in the middle of each table, and each person can add up what she thinks the total cost represented is. Cans of cleanser would be appropriate for prizes.

3. Is there a missionary available to share what is happening today to alleviate the suffering of lepers?

4. Share some memories of those who have lived in military housing situations.

Eight
Home in the City

1. Explore resources within your own city for enriching the quality of life, as well as to discover avenues of service.

2. Invite a member of your local library staff to inform your group as to its widening sphere of services.

3. Make inquiries to your local chamber of commerce as to projects that are being undertaken to make your city more beautiful.

4. A tax consultant might be a good resource guest for questions and answers!

5. Just for fun, give a prize to the shortest person present—and another to the one with the most tax deductions.

6. Weather permitting, meet out under the trees.

7. Introduce or close your session with the reading of the tract "If Jesus Came to Your House." (See Never Underestimate the Power of God's Woman, by Daisy Hepburn.)

Nine
Home in the Country

1. Let this be a country fair day with each one bringing a homemade article for display and then for a silent auction.

2. Check with your public library or other resource for movies on rural America, harvesttime, canning foods, or some other item of interest having to do with country living.

Ten
Home in Heaven

1. A special musical program featuring "heavenly songs" and ones of hope would be a delightful introduction to this lesson.

2. Enjoy a tidbit tasting refreshment time sampling heavenly dishes, supplying recipes for a repeat at home. (This might be a useful idea for raising funds as the recipes are sold.)

3. Since this is the last lesson in this series, a talent festival—vocal, instrumental, and displays of special crafts and art work could create a gala event.

4. Invite a qualified person to review one of the newer books written on death and dying from a Christian perspective. (Your Christian bookstore can make some recommendations.)

21
BE MINE

"Be Mine" is your guide to a creative study of the book of Ruth. The study is designed to increase your understanding of this remarkable Old Testament story, especially as it illustrates many New Testament promises.

The studies are organized to be used in either four or five sessions. The questions are excellent for group discussion and no other teacher's guide is necessary. Be very sure that everyone using this study has individual access to the Bible.

In whatever way you use "Be Mine," it is my prayer that as you look at Ruth's love story you will grow in awareness of the special love relationship that you have with Jesus Christ.

Here is Your Name Tag.
Photocopy and color it. Then staple a bit of grosgrain ribbon to the top, so that it will last longer, and can be used throughout this study.

A Family Affair

Person	Characteristics of Person		What God Allowed	Person's Reaction	Leading Lesson from This Life
	Good	Bad			
Elimelech (God is king)					
Mahlon and Chilion (Sickly and pining)					
Naomi (Pleasant, God is sweet)					
Orpha					
Ruth (Faithful friend)					
Boaz (Strength)					

22
COLOR ME CHRISTIAN

Preparing for this Study:
1. Use the reading of Marjorie Holmes, entitled "Colors", from her book *I've Got to Talk to Somebody, God,* published by Bantam Books (available in libraries).

2. Invite the ladies to write a reading or prayer of their own, or paraphrase a psalm, reflecting on the colors in their lives.

Ideas for making your get-togethers colorful:
1. Arrange your meeting place so that the ladies can sit around tables—this makes for good fellowship!

2. Use a game or puzzle as an icebreaker—felt tipped markers or "crayon candles" make good prizes.

3. Invite the ladies to wear the color of the week or month when they come to the get-together.

4. Arrange groups of articles (all the same color) as table centerpieces. Let different women bring the centerpiece each time, allowing opportunity for them to share at their tables some history of their collection—everything from candy and fruit to an unusual scarf, planter, or toy! Imagination is the only limitation!

5. Be sure to have a glass or two (or covered tin can) with felt tipped markers on each table for coloring/doodling name tags and craft items. (There will be those who will be hard to convince that this is worthwhile—try it—I promise you it works!)

6. Invest in spools of inexpensive satin ribbon in rainbow colors. The ribbon is effective in large showy bows for plants, table runners, prize packages, as well as more ambitious "canopy creating" for a special brunch or Color Me Christian luncheon. For a beautiful and relatively simple canopy, install two wires above the area of program focus. Lay (or attach with tape) ribbons in rainbow order on rear wire and drape them across front wire. Round the end of each ribbon for a scalloped edge.

7. This is an ideal time to encourage the women to read. Set up a book table, featuring biographies of the women who have colored our world.

Icebreaker:
Reproduce copies of the following icebreaker.
See if you can find someone who qualifies for one of the following and invite her to write her name on the line that fits. Try to get acquainted with someone new to you!

1. My name has a color in it _____
2. I brought a red purse _____
3. I had orange juice for breakfast _____
4. Notice my blue eyes _____
5. My wallet is blue _____
6. My hair is naturally gray _____
7. I have pink nail polish on _____
8. I have some purple on _____
9. My thumb is green (meaning I have more than a dozen plants in my home!) _____
10. Rah! I was a high school cheerleader! _____

Make each get-together a colorful creation:

1. Make name tags to be worn at each meeting and arrange one table in each rainbow color.

2. Introduce the Bible women from this first lesson by asking some ladies to dress as these characters (Allow them to enter with some music and drama! One small spotlight works wonders.) and tell a bit about themselves, highlighting their color quality. Encourage participation by taking a poll to see if the audience agrees with the ideas presented to them.

3. Since it is suggested that you find an unsecret pal until the next get-together and perhaps even making some goodies for her, why not have a recipe exchange?

4. Invite a guest to give the women information on current concerns. Even provide stationery for letters to be written to TV networks and sponsors expressing concern. A panel discussion on "How to Help" is appropriate.

5. Good News Publishers in Westchester, Illinois (9825 W. Roosevelt Road, 60153) printed a tract by Corrie tenBoom called *I'm Still Learning to Forgive.* Why not purchase one for each lady?

6. Create a skit/interview with Fanny Crosby. (Note the script following.) Or invite a musician to share Crosby hymns with the group. Make *music*!

7. The Salvation Army in your community will be glad to help you with resources for Catherine Booth. Many current films are available to introduce your group to the evangelistic organization and its work.

8. Queen for a Day is everyone at your get-together. Prepare a little takeoff on the old television program—just for fun—when the contestants told their troubles to see whose was worst. Remember that she was elected queen for the day and given prizes. Don't forget a robe and crown. Or it could be a surprise day for someone you would like to honor.

Whatever you do—make every get together memorable!

An Interview with Fanny Crosby

We welcome you into the tiny New England apartment of a lady who has been known as "Queen of Gospel Song." The year is 1904 and Fanny is eighty-four. She is a tiny woman, less than five feet tall, and weighs less than 100 pounds. Because her first concern is people and their life in Christ, she has consented to give us this time. Let's join her:

It seems, Miss Crosby, that at last Americans are beginning to discover the composer behind the thousands of hymns that we sing in our churches today bearing your name.

Good day. Well, it was never my intention to promote Fanny Crosby. The Lord Jesus Christ is my Saviour and the Giver of every good and perfect gift. All praise and power go to Him.
Tell us a little about your early life in Christ. Was your parental home a Christian one?

Oh, my, yes! We went to church every Sunday, although the services were very long and boring to me. I was already in my teens before I think I had my own special experience with the Lord and became converted and committed to Him.

We have heard that you have a remarkable memory and that by the age of ten you had memorized the entire Pentateuch, all four Gospels, the Proverbs, Ruth, the Song of Solomon and many of the Psalms. Is that possibly true?

Yes. I know that it seems that God gave me a special memory, but He gives everyone this ability, I feel. Most people who have eyes lose it through laziness.

Were you able to go to school as a child?

My dear mother, who had to work so hard to support me since my father died so young, tried to enroll me in school near our home. It was so discouraging for me, though, that I gave up time after time. Then, when I was fourteen I heard of the New York Institute for the Blind. It was one of the happiest days of my life.

You had to move into New York City to attend this school. It must have been quite an adjustment for you.

It was an adjustment, but the excitement of the opportunity was almost more than I could stand. If I could have imagined then where God was going to take me . . . At the institute I traveled after classes with groups of students as we shared the story of our school, and the fact that blind people could be taught. That was news in those days and we were considered an oddity. I stayed at the school for several years, even becoming an instructor, and later dean of students. I even served as a nurse during the terrible cholera epidemic.

You met someone very important to you at the school. Right?

How did you know? My husband, Van, who was a blind teacher of music. Van gave music lessons to poor children and worked as a paid organist to support us. We became especially concerned about the poor and moved into a tenement in lower New York City in order to minister to them. Many of my songs were written so that they could understand the simplest gospel, and express their love for Jesus.

Did you have any children, Fanny?

Yes, God gave us a tender babe. But, each of us has some things that are very personal and private of which we do not speak openly to others. We loved our infant dearly, but soon the angels came down and took our child back to God. Although I cannot tell you any more about this, let me say that I wrote probably my favorite of all these hymns, "Safe in the Arms of Jesus," just for mothers who had lost children.

You have mentioned writing for the poor and for mothers, but I understand that you supplied hundreds of hymns for some famous evangelists and preachers.

Mr. Dwight L. Moody became a special friend, as well as his singer, Ira Sankey. God blessed us all during those years, and He gave me nearly nine thousand hymns. Of course, not all of them were published.

Tell us, Fanny, do you feel any bitterness or animosity toward the doctor who caused the blindness?

Mother told me that because he put such a strong poultice on my eyes they were injured, causing my blindness. Of course, I have wondered what my life might have been like if I could have seen, but the doctor didn't intentionally harm me. If I could meet him, I would tell him that he really gave me a gift. My lack of sight has been more than compensated for by my soul's vision.

*This is my story, this is my song
Praising my Savior all the day long.*

9. Now end the get-together with some colorful singing.

Sing this prayer together to the tune of "Beautiful Dreamer".

    Beautiful Saviour, Thou didst impart
    Thy wondrous cleansing to my sinful heart;
    Thy Holy Spirit dwelling within
    Restores my soul to Thy likeness again.

    (chorus)
    Beautiful Saviour, may others see
    Thy likeness always reflected through me;
    O keep me pure and looking above
    That I may radiate Thy perfect love!
    That I may radiate Thy perfect love!

    Make me a portrait, Saviour Divine,
    Of all the graces that truly are Thine;
    May many souls be drawn unto Thee
    Because they shall see Thee living through me.

This simple praise song is sung to the tune of "Edelweiss."

    Praise the Lord, Praise the Lord,
    Praise the Lord, alleluia (repeat)
    King of kings and Lord of lords
    Praise His name forever,
    Praise the Lord, Praise the Lord, Praise the Lord, alleluia!

        —Joan Guldenschuh

23
CONSIDER CHRIST

This booklet has been prepared for use by women who want to learn and grow and want to provide group study and worship. Use the questions for discussion and the songs and poems for praise and prayer.

These are simple studies of the seven women who were near the cross of Jesus. It is my prayer that you might find yourself drawn closer to the Christ of the cross as a result of the time you spend in His Word.

Consider that possibility!

The spiritual truths revealed in the seven Bible studies in "Consider Christ" can find creative expression in a get-together for women. Let the gatherings show how God's truth can be expressed in women's lives.

The suggested activities will lead women into new relationships and prepare them for involvement with God in a new relationship. These gatherings are not a new women's program in the church, but rather a series of get-togethers where the unexpected happens each time.

With imagination, the main concept of each Bible study can be captured in a craft item to take home and keep as a reminder. The Scripture passages may suggest a centerpiece idea, a theme for decorations, or an idea for refreshments. You may use an icebreaker activity that will convey an important idea in a meaningful, memorable way. Choose crafts and activities that require a maximum of sharing opportunities and let everyone be seated comfortably and informally.

Aim for variety. There need not be a craft project during every get-together. Perhaps one study might suggest a praise celebration in the form of a concert. Whatever you plan, let each gathering be a very special consideration.

One
Mary, His Mother

Consider Mary and her family relationship to Christ Himself.

Using the concept of family relationships, create a get-together that expresses the spiritual truths of this first Bible study in the "Consider Christ" series.

Have participants bring: a twiggy branch, small pictures of family members and a Bible.

Have ready to use: name tags for each participant (see figure 21), a record, a stereo, song sheets, white spray paint, Styrofoam ball halves, ribbon, straw flowers, information and a prize for the game.

A family tree might depict family relationships to make a lasting, effective craft. Each person arrives, picks up her name tag, then sprays her branch white and anchors it in half a Styrofoam ball.

While the branches dry, serve coffee and goodies. The song "All God's Children" from Bill Gaither's record might be played in the background. Use this as an introduction to the first Bible study, which should then be shared and discussed for about forty-five minutes.

Close the study with another Gaither song, "The Family of God"—using small song sheets decorated with a sketch of a Family Tree.

Now take up the branches and complete your family trees. Supply pre-cut pieces of narrow velvet ribbon and a few straw flowers. Let the women tie their pictures onto the trees with the ribbon, inserting flowers into the bows of those who are already members of God's family. The tree can serve as a prayer reminder. In fact, after the trees are completed, take a few minutes to pray for each family represented.

Just for fun, before leaving, give a small prize to the one who can come closest to guessing how many numbers are listed in your local phone book under one family name. Be sure to select a common name and know the number ahead of time. A good prize might be an address book.

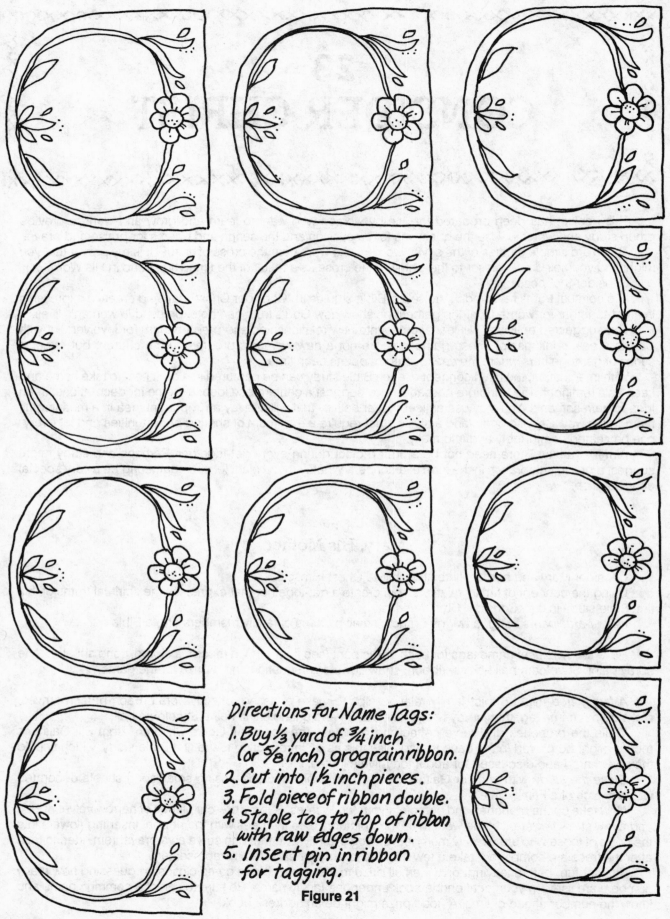

Directions for Name Tags:
1. Buy ⅓ yard of ¾ inch
   (or ⅝ inch) grograin ribbon.
2. Cut into 1½ inch pieces.
3. Fold piece of ribbon double.
4. Staple tag to top of ribbon
   with raw edges down.
5. Insert pin in ribbon
   for tagging.

Figure 21

Two
Salome, Mother of James and John

Consider Salome, the wife and mother of fishermen. Fishermen suggest fish. Imagine what you can do with fish at a women's get-together.

Have participants bring: Bible.

Have ready to use: name tags, centerpieces, felt, fish patterns, plastic eyes, typed Scripture verses and magnetic tape.

Refreshment idea: tuna sandwiches or shrimp salad.

Have everyone catch a fish name tag as she enters the door. Use goldfish bowls with live fish for centerpieces. When everyone's seated, bring in coffee and tunafish sandwiches. If you care to eat with style, serve shrimp salad.

Involve everyone in conversation and the Bible study with the making of a magnetic fish at each table. Use a small piece of felt cut in the shape of a fish, a small moveable plastic eye, and the key verse found in Ephesians 2:6 typed out on a square of paper to glue on the fish. Apply a ½-inch strip of magnetic tape to the back of the fish. Now everyone has a Scripture reminder for the refrigerator or car dashboard!

Because Salome was concerned about her sons' position in Christ's kingdom, have everyone bring pictures of their sons—and daughters. Tape these around the room on the walls. When the fish are completed, tour the room with pencil and paper in hand to guess whose children are whose.

For fun, tell fish stories around your table. Award the goldfish bowl to the one with the biggest fish story. You might have three of the best tell their tale to the whole group—in sixty seconds or less.

Shift the focus of high spirits to a joyful united song—maybe a verse or two of "Blessed Assurance" because you can be sure of your position in Christ.

Then open your booklet to the second Bible study and spend forty-five minutes considering your position in Christ.

Be sure to stop and spend a few minutes in prayer on behalf of your children.

Three
Consider Your Devotion to Christ

Consider Mary of Bethany and devotion to Christ.

Three ways in which you can express your devotion to Christ, through your get-together, are Bible study, prayer and praise.

Have participants bring: a Bible.

Have ready to use: centerpieces, a prepared poem reading, name tags that match the table places, song sheets, mini concert arrangements, and prayer promises.

Refreshment ideas: what would Mary of Bethany have done?

Suggest these three aspects of the devotional life in table centerpieces of live green plants (depicting growth in Christ), with a Bible, praying hands, and a musical note cut from greeting cards or seals "growing" on chenille stems from the plant.

Divide your get-together into three parts. Begin with Bible study, using the third lesson in the "Consider Christ" series. Select someone beforehand to introduce the study by reading from the booklet the poem "Crowded Out" as part of her devotions. Have her seated in a kitchen chair, with apron on, coffee cup in hand and her Bible on a table beside her. After the poem, have her share the meaning of daily devotional time in her life, emphasizing the three aspects mentioned above.

During the second part of your meeting, spend time in conversational prayer around your tables. A possible introduction might be to share prayer requests and prayer promises for answers.

(A reference for a prayer promise from the Bible should be printed on each name tag. Each person can find her place at the table by matching the reference on her name tag with a lettered verse at each place.

These are easily done by purchasing a box of Scripture promises which can double as place cards.)

The last part can be a celebration of praise with singing. Invite someone from your group or a guest to sing or play an instrument. Mimeograph song sheets or praise songs so everyone can "make a joyful noise unto the Lord."

Close with the reading of the poem, "A Heart to Praise Thee," found in their study books.

Four
Martha of Bethany

Consider Martha and how she served Christ. Service is the concept to express creatively through your get-together. Let a tray be the object to convey the idea.

Have participants bring: their Bible and scissors.

Have ready to use: name tags, supplies for making simple tray favors and a variety of prepared trays.

Refreshment idea: tray snacks and coffee.

At the door, have everyone choose her name tag from a tray. Have hostesses carry trays to the tables and serve the women coffee and goodies individually.

There are so many ways to serve. To demonstrate a few, several women may bring in different types of trays to set on the tables as centerpieces. One could be a TV tray with recipes and samples of snacks to be passed around. Another could be a cleaning tray with supplies you carry around for housework. Another could be a "sunshine" tray for a sickbed—with flowers, get-well cards and books to be read. This might be a time for a short review of an appropriate book for a shut-in. A fourth might be a tea tray with an antique tea service for entertaining guests.

Let someone within your group compose some poetry for this parade of trays, adding others you might think of.

Then, allow everyone to be of service by making simple tray favors to be delivered to a hospital or nursing home. This is always a welcome gift!

Allow thirty to forty-five minutes to consider your service to Christ by doing Bible study four in the "Consider Christ" studies.

Conclude with prayer and the poem "Keep Sweet," found in the booklet.

Five
Mary of Magdala

Consider Mary, and that Christ set her free from that which bound her. He can set you free from whatever limitations or problems that bind you.

Celebrate freedom in Him at your get-together.

Have participants bring: old magazines, scissors, and a Bible.

Have ready to use: poster board, felt pens, glue, prizes, string, paper for name tags, and song sheets.

Begin your celebration by making posters to advertise your need for freedom. Provide each table with a half sheet of poster board, marking pens, scissors, glue, and several magazines. Give the group fifteen minutes to express in words and pictures what they particularly want to be liberated from.

Choose a representative from each table to bring the poster to the front and be ready to interpret its significance. Display the posters across the front wall—even consider a protest march! By applause vote, select the most convincing poster and give a prize to the winning group. How about appropriate car bumper stickers available at your local Christian bookstore?

May the chains that bind in slavery be broken, but blest be the tie that binds in love.

To introduce the Bible study, make a prayer chain.

Have everyone write their name on a 4" × 1" piece of colored paper as they enter, then pin these on for name tags. At this point, take off the name tags, and have each table make a paper chain, linking these papers together. Depending on the size of the group, perhaps just one long chain can be made, each resolving to keep the chain intact as she prays for those with whom she is linked (at least until the next meeting).

Consider freedom in Christ by studying Mary of Magdala in Bible study five in "Consider Christ." Celebrate your freedom with a special closing song such as "He Touched Me" and prayer.

Six
Claudia Procula

Consider Claudia, a woman of influence and married to a politician. She had the opportunity to influence her husband. So do you!

Have participants bring: a friend to hear the guest speaker and a Bible.

Have ready to use: lawn posters, centerpieces and prizes.
Refreshment idea: something special for guests.

Let the husbands play the role of political candidates for this get-together. Why not prepare some campaign posters to affix to stakes and place on the lawn outside of your meeting place. Let them promote such ideas as "SUPPORT OUR MAN" "HE'S #1" "WIN WITH OUR MAN" or any other that would incite curiosity and conversation as the women enter!

You might celebrate marriage by making centerpieces depicting anniversaries—wood for five years, china for twenty, or silver or gold. As the women enter, let those who have been married one to five years sit at one table, those from ten to nineteen at another, etc. Be sure to have a "singles" table and let them create their own centerpiece, depicting their areas of influence and careers (perhaps a nurse's cap, schoolbooks for teachers, etc.). Create a simple icebreaker game with anniversaries in mind.

Let this be a get-together with a guest speaker. Invite the wife of a Christian man, who has been elected to some office in the community, to share her experiences and responsibilities in this role. It might be the wife of a school board official or a member of the state or local government.
This study is one of the best for discussion, so be sure to allow sufficient time for at least thirty minutes to be spent with Bibles and study books around the various tables. The fact that the women have been grouped according to years married will affect the discussion—and should make it more interesting.

Seven
Cleopas's Wife

Consider walking with Christ through your daily life.

Have participants bring: their Bibles.
Have ready to use: name tags, road maps, centerpieces, song sheets, and a slide presentation.

Name tags should be in the shape of footprints. Spread road maps in the centers of tables. Spray-paint discarded shoes, fill with greens or dried flowers and use for centerpieces.

Over a cup of coffee, allow about ten minutes to discover a place in each other's lives where your paths have crossed. This can be a real discovery and friendship renewer.

Sing songs, medley-style—"Where He Leads Me"; "Following Jesus"; "Walking with Jesus"; and "All the Way My Savior Leads"—or others you might think of.

Discover someone who has been to the Holy Land to give a fifteen-minute slide presentation accompanied by the music "I Walked Today Where Jesus Walked."

Complete your book by sharing study seven in "Consider Christ" and close with the song "O Master Let Me Walk with Thee" and prayer.

24
GET UP AND GO

As you read through "Get Up and Go," you will see that the Bible studies vary in length. Use them to your own best advantage.

Be sure to consider the following ideas for making your get-togethers an event.

You will have many other ideas as you see the Word of God come alive in you.

Celebrate—and may God bless you richly.

One

1. Create some signposts for centerpieces. Poster board copies of "Get Up and Go" will be easy to mount on a dowel stick and put in half a Styrofoam ball. Use several, including a "one way" sign!

2. Make copies of a map leaving out names of cities or other landmarks, and number some spots for the women to identify in a given time. An atlas or road map might be the prize.

3. Have someone report on what is happening to the Church of Jesus Christ behind the Iron Curtain right now. Perhaps a book report on *Beyond the Wall*, by Hank Paulsen with Don Richardson, could be made.

4. Announce a project to set the first four verses of Psalm 90 to music. Invite the women to bring back their song next time. Suggest they use a familiar tune and phrases from the Scripture.

5. There are exercises at the end of "Get Up and Go" section. Do one or several each time you get together. This will help everyone's get-up-and-go!

Two

1. This lesson might be introduced with a short "This Is Your Life, Moses" skit. Be sure to have participants dress the part. Create the skit along the line of the old TV program with people from Moses' past surprising him with stories of their part in his life.

2. This get-together is a good time for a baby shower for a missionary project. Perhaps a layette could be assembled for someone special.

3. Centerpieces could be breadbaskets with dolls wrapped in flannel inside.

4. *Make a favor:*
   (1) Cut with pinking shears, a 4-inch triangle of pastel-print fabric.
   (2) Dip into melted paraffin (which has been melted in a double-boiler for safety).
   (3) Shape quickly into diaper, pin into place and "set" on foil. It will quickly dry and become a "cup" for candies or nuts.

Three

1. Let this get-together be a time to introduce conversational prayer. Allow the women to form small groups (from five to ten in each group) and talk to God. Perhaps you will want to suggest some prayer topics.

2. Encourage someone to look up the little book *Practicing the Presence of God*, by Brother Laurence, and give a brief report on this saintly man's "ordinariness."

3. Perhaps centerpieces could be brightly blooming plants, to suggest a burning bush.

4. Or, have arrangements of several candles of various heights in the centers of the tables, with greens grouped at the bases.

5. Create a candleholder as follows: Glue four clay pigeons together. Paint if desired. Set a chimney glass on top pigeon, placing a thick candle inside. Tie a gingham ribbon around the candlestand and add a few straw flowers.

Four

1. Arrange a table containing the newest in Christian books on the subject of "The Christian Women's Liberation." There have been many written in the last few years, and it would be helpful to not only review several but to even supply a booklist (this could be procured at a Christian bookstore).

2. For those who feel sometimes like slaves to housework (short of making bricks!) arrange a demonstration on cleaning tips. Household hints are always welcome.

3. Appoint a Sunshine Committee, before the next get-together, to visit those who are housebound. Be sure and choose only those free spirited ones who would consider it a privilege!

4. Just for fun—make a frog beanbag. Suggest that the women bring scraps of polyester knit fabric, scissors and a needle and thread. Using the pattern (see figure 24), cut fabric, stitch and fill with birdseed before closing. Glue or tack on eyes.

5. To be thrown when feeling *plagued*—or given away!

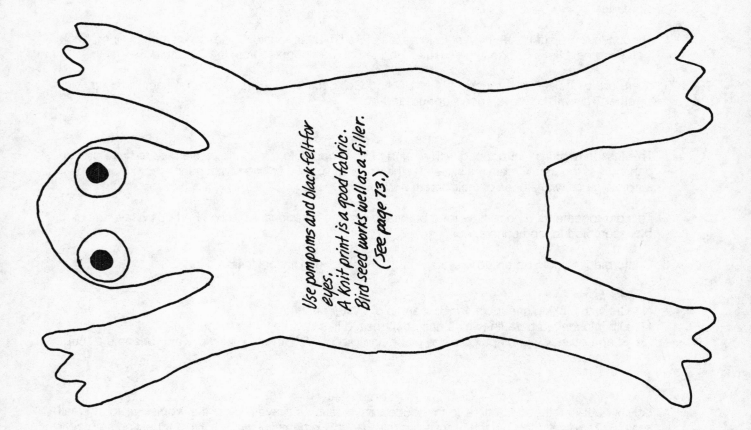

Use pompoms and black felt for eyes. A knit print is a good fabric. Bird seed works well as a filler. (See page 73.)

Figure 24

Five

1. Crosses made of twigs are appropriate centerpieces for this get-together.

2. A small bundle of twigs or weeds symbolizing our faith might be laid alongside the cross. The twigs are like the hyssop which was dipped into the blood to be applied to the doorposts.

3. Have a time of singing. Choose the songs which reinforce the salvation plan.

4. Let your refreshments be the items on the Passover menu. You might want to eat this quietly, even in candlelight with a musical and scriptural background. Let the hostesses be in simple biblical dress.

5. Allow time for the women to share what it is they have to celebrate. Pray that God will help each one to be able to witness to her own salvation experience.

Six

1. Create your own praise gathering. Invite some special music to visit your get-together.

2. Play a little "Name That Tune," with someone playing parts of some old hymns on the piano. Give a prize that needs water to activate it, i.e., tea bags, lemonade, Koolaid, etc.

3. Encourage the women to share praise promises and prayer together.

4. It is an ideal time to have a women's chorus ready to sing. Music for Miriam's song of praise is available in a modern Scripture-set-to-music songbook.

5. Just for fun, why not make big poster boards Cs and set them in slits carved in half Styrofoam balls for centerpieces.

6. Supply some familiar tunes, and let groups of three make songs of their own to be sung for the group after a given length of time. Ten minutes is plenty.

Seven

1. Centerpieces might be popcorn in various size canning jars (at least three on each table) with a bright bow around the neck of the jar (manna). Or, dried loaves of unsliced bread, which have been varnished and then tied up with gingham ribbon and straw flowers.

2. Have ideas for new recipes for breads or sandwiches. This could be an appealing demonstration.

3. According to Psalm 78:25, why not serve angel food cake with some variation, for refreshments.

4. To further develop an appreciation for bread or manna, why not have a "Price Is Right" game with bread. Buy three or four loaves of unusual bread and allow the women to write down their guess for the collective price. The ones coming closest will each receive a loaf of the bread.

5. Allow the ambitious ones to try their hand at some bread dough art.

Eight

1. Let this be a family reunion. Invite everyone to bring family pictures. You may want to create a game by numbering the pictures and allowing the women to identify the families involved. (Give a picture frame for a prize.)

2. Since this is also a lesson in priorities, invite the women to come to this get-together with a report in writing on how their time was spent in the previous week. Allow time for discussing ways they could better schedule their day's activities.

3. Have at least two or three women try to bring with them the one who most influenced them to Christ. Some personal witness would be encouraging.

Nine

1. Heart-shaped cakes with decorated "Tablets of Law" in the center of the table makes a delicious and meaningful centerpiece.

2. Supply some magazines and scissors, construction paper and glue. In pairs, invite the women to illustrate one of the commandments, then tape them to the wall around the room (after about ten minutes) and let each try to identify the commandment.

3. I have found some "DID YOU KNOW IT WAS LAW" place mats, at a local paper company. This information is available at your library. Why not make your own lists of true and false quiz items on what is actually law in your state. Consider duplicating the game and let it double as a place mat.

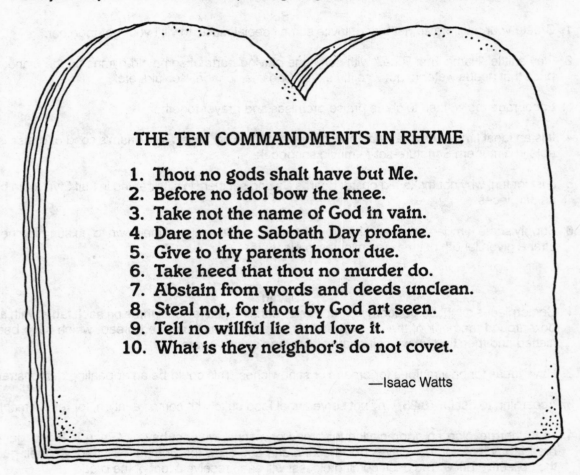

THE TEN COMMANDMENTS IN RHYME

1. Thou no gods shalt have but Me.
2. Before no idol bow the knee.
3. Take not the name of God in vain.
4. Dare not the Sabbath Day profane.
5. Give to thy parents honor due.
6. Take heed that thou no murder do.
7. Abstain from words and deeds unclean.
8. Steal not, for thou by God art seen.
9. Tell no willful lie and love it.
10. What is they neighbor's do not covet.

—Isaac Watts

Ten

1. Use white tablecloths with red, blue, and purple flowers or ribbons (the colors of the Tabernacle).

2. Create a simple worship center significant of the Holy Place, using a praying hands model, a basket or tray of bread, and a candlestick.

3. Provide squares of white linen with red, purple, and blue embroidery thread. A transfer pencil outlining the letters of Psalm 122:1, and ironed on to the linen can be embroidered. The verse can then be framed by the women at home.

4. Have a time of worship, including singing of hymns, prayer, and a Scripture reading. You might want to use the responsive reading (following) to take a worship walk through the Tabernacle.

A Worship Walk Through the Tabernacle
(to be read responsively)

Leader: Let us enter into His gate with thanksgiving, and into His courts with praise.

Response: I am the door: by me if any man enter in, he shall be saved, and shall go in and out, and find pasture.

Leader: Let us meet Him at the altar of forgiveness. We have an altar, the cross where Christ was sacrificed.

Response: If we confess our sins, he is faithful and just to forgive us our sins, and to cleanse us from all unrighteousness.

Leader: Move on with Him to the place of cleansing. For who shall ascend into the hill of the Lord? or who shall stand in His holy place?

Response: He that hath clean hands, and a pure heart. Cleanse thou me from secret faults. Wash me and I shall be whiter than snow.

Leader: Inside this place of worship there were two rooms. The first one contained the golden candlestick and a table with special loaves of holy bread upon it. There was an altar of incense.

Response: And so, dear friends, let us go right in to the Holy of Holies where God is, because of the blood of Jesus. This is the fresh, new, life-giving way which Christ has opened up for us by tearing the curtain—His human body—to let us into the holy presence of God.

All: Now we can look forward to the salvation God has promised us. There is no longer any room for doubt, and we can tell others that salvation is ours, for there is no question that He will do what He says.

Selected portions of Scripture Psalm 100, John 10, Psalm 24, Hebrews 9 and 10, 1 John 1.)

Some Exercises for People on the Go:
(Do one or two at each get-together—with gusto!)

1. *Jump-ups:* Stand, feet together, arms at sides. Count one—jump with feet apart and clap hands over head. Count two—return to standing position. Repeat 10 times.

2. *Toner:* Stride standing position, hands on hips. Bending from the waist, bend forward, side, back and side, using four counts. Do 10 times.

3. *Relaxer:* Stride standing position, let arms and upper part of body relax forward and downward, then raise up to standing position and stretch arms toward ceiling. Repeat 10 times.

4. *Whirl:* Stride stand, arms raised sideways shoulder high. Moving from the shoulder, circle arms backwards and forward in small circles 8 times and relax. Repeat four times.

5. *Kick-Swing:* Stand with one side to wall or chair and hold on with one hand. Kick or swing outside leg forward and back 10 times, moving from the hip. Repeat 10 times.

6. *Trimmer:* An isometric or resistive exercise. Stride stand—put palms of hands together in front of chest. Push palms together hard, and at the same time, pull in abdominal muscles as tightly as possible. Fingers should be pointed upward. Count to eight, and relax, and repeat four times.

7. *Flexor:* Stand, feet together, arms at sides. Keep feet flat on floor, do half deep-knee bend, at same time raising arms forward and up to shoulder height. Back to standing position and repeat 10 times.

8. *Lifter:* Stand, toes pointing inward and heels out. Do heel raising and lowering 10 times.

—Sandy Abramson By permission

25
GET UP AND GROW

Tips on the cultivation of a Christian, including Bible studies and creative program aids.

This study is designed with you in mind for—

     a neighborhood ministry

     a church women's organization

     a small group Bible study

     a retreat

with the concept of involvement for everyone thereby reinforcing the truth of the Word of God.

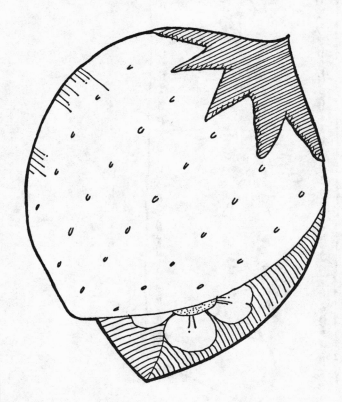

Here is Your Name Tag.
Photocopy and color it. Then staple a bit of grosgrain ribbon to the top, so that it will last longer, and can be used throughout this study.

One
A Time for Planting

1. Use green tablecloths and accent napkins.

2. Centerpieces might be seed jars prepared ahead of time or live green plants brought from homes.

3. For a starter—on a dozen or so pieces of construction paper, glue a few seeds of a familiar variety. Tape these to the walls and give the women a few minutes to see if they can identify the fruit or vegetable that will result from the seed sample. You will need packets of seeds, of course, for prizes.

4. Creating simple seed pictures on natural burlap ribbon offers an opportunity for involvement (see figure 25).

5. Just for fun look for the page on "Gardening from the Garbage" in the study book. Maybe some women could bring some fruit seeds to plant.

6. A simple planter may be made for each member to take home her plant. Use old-fashioned clothes pins and one tuna fish can. Have a folded piece of paper around the top of the can to make it thick enough for clamping the clothes pins. Fit the pins tightly slanting sideways. It is not necessary to glue. Spray with a bring color and enjoy.

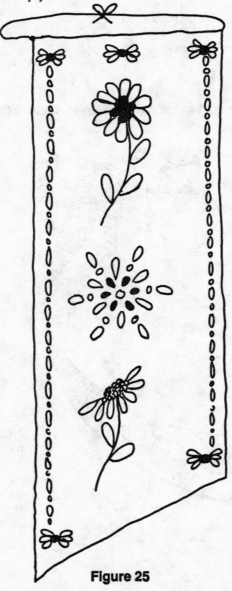

Figure 25

Two
A Time for Cultivating

1. Indoor gardening tools can be centerpieces with new ones to be given as prizes. Use brown table-cloths this time. Share or trade plant slips for home cultivation.

2. Begin working on embroidery items.

3. A brief object lesson using the prayer plant should introduce the prayer time at this session.

4. Invite someone from a garden club to speak briefly on the care and feeding of house plants.

Three
A Time for Weeding

Dried weed bundles for centerpieces can be used. Invite the women to bring containers from home and create dry flower or weed arrangements together.

Four
A Time for Pruning

1. Grapes and ivy are appropriate centerpieces. Even branches anchored in plaster, either sprayed or left naturally bare, are attractive.

2. Is there someone locally who might be able to give some information on crafting, or pruning for greater blossoms or fruit? Maybe it could be someone who would be surprised to learn of the scriptural authority for his trade.

Five
A Time for Harvesting

1. Use fruit baskets for centerpieces. Why not have a recipe exchange on new ways to serve the fruits. Reinforce the fact that the harvest is to be shared!
2. Special music for this occasion might include songs of thanksgiving and praise. God will keep His Word as we abide in Him—the harvest is to be enjoyed.

26
LIVING SIMPLY

In this preshrunk, stretch-to-fit, one-size-fits-all world a pattern seems to be unfolding—a pattern for living simply, and it fits me best of all!

Often, in a concerted effort to cope, life becomes so complicated that it is easy to feel as if there is no basic pattern provided. Will it all turn out all right? Can we really be satisfied with the way things are getting put together?

Jesus is our Model. Our instructions are clearly and simply stated in the Word of God. Perhaps the pattern in Living Simply, found in the Bible, will be helpful as you look to the One who sees the fabric of your life already woven, complete and beautifully put together.

Special guest: Consider inviting someone from a local fabric store or sewing center for a demonstration on fabric care or some other facet of sewing.

Name tags: Use a threaded needle to fasten the name tags to the ladies' lapels or dresses.

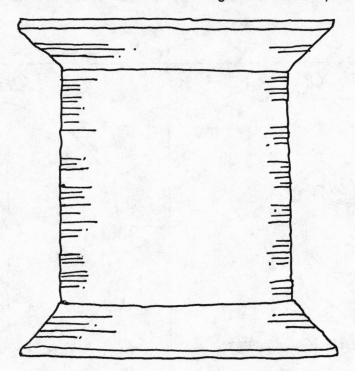

Decorations: Your imagination is required to create the setting with fabric remnants for tablecloths, sewing baskets and dress forms for decoration. Use irons for centerpieces for "Keep Referring to the Pattern," with a large cardboard tag tied to the cord reading "Cheer Up and Press On."

Correlated crafts for each lesson follow.

These lessons have been assembled with prayer that they will "fit you" and suit your special style. Embarrassingly, I have found that my most noticeable sewing disasters have occurred because I forgot to remember to look it all over first, then follow the instructions. *"See that you make all things according to the pattern shown to you"* (Heb. 8:5, KJV).

Book Cover

Personalized cut out
Personalized cut out

1. Lay out book on fabric – felt or non-raveling material.
2. Allow 2" fold back on each side.
3. Cut ½" wider at top and bottom.
4. Sew 2" in at top and bottom, ½" deep.
5. Applique or glue on apple made from felt or other fabric.
6. Personalize by writing your name on cut out.
7. Attach short ties if desired.

Place Mat

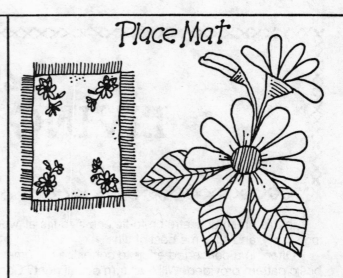

1. Cut mat approximately 12"x15" from burlap loosely woven fabric.
2. Fringe at least ½" on all sides.
3. Trace florals in each corner.
4. Embroider with yarn in satin and lazy daisy stitches.
5. Don't attempt to make each corner identical.

Pincushion

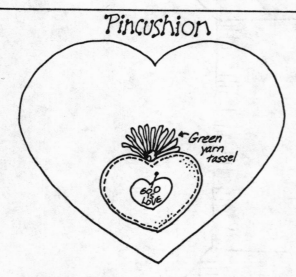

Green yarn tassel

GOD IS LOVE

1. Cut two hearts from red felt with pinking shears (if available).
2. Sew around edges, (by hand or machine) or use fabric glue, leaving opening for stuffing.
3. Stuff with one nylon hose or stuffing of your choice.
4. Close opening.
5. Make tassel: wrap yarn around a paper tube ten times. Tie, cut and attach to top of heart.
6. Tie two of the yarn strands together for a loop to hang.
7. Cut out and pin on "GOD IS LOVE."

Banner

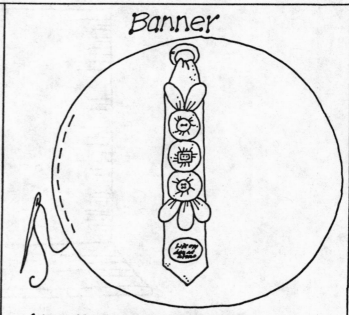

1. Cut strip of felt (gold, etc.), 12" long by 2" wide.
2. Cut three circles (using pattern) of assorted fabric, five circles of green fabric.
3. Sew running stitch ¼" around edge; pull thread snugly for gathers and knot. Flatten with gathers in center for flower, pull to peak to make leaf.
4. Sew one button in center of each flower. Arrange on felt with leaves. Sew or glue.
5. Glue cutout on bottom and attach curtain ring on top, folding over felt; sew or glue.

Cut-Outs

Live one day at a time.

GOD LOVES

God will help you keep on growing.

Print in your name with permanent ink.

GOD IS LOVE

LOVE

PEACE

JOY

Cut out any picture from light weight paper (and your name or initials). Attach to bucket with clear contact paper.

Hanging

Place on fold.

Place on fold.

1. Cut burlap or similar fabric 7"x12". Make point by folding back bottom corners; press and glue.
2. Glue on screen molding or sew casing for doweling; 8" long.
3. Attach yarn or cord.
4. Draw stems and heart (see pincushion pattern) with permanent markers.
5. Sew buttons on top of stems.
6. Cut out three flowers and three leaves. (Use patterns.)
7. Slit flowers to fit on buttons. Glue on leaves. Glue cut-out on drawn heart.

Place on fold.

LEAF
Place on fold.

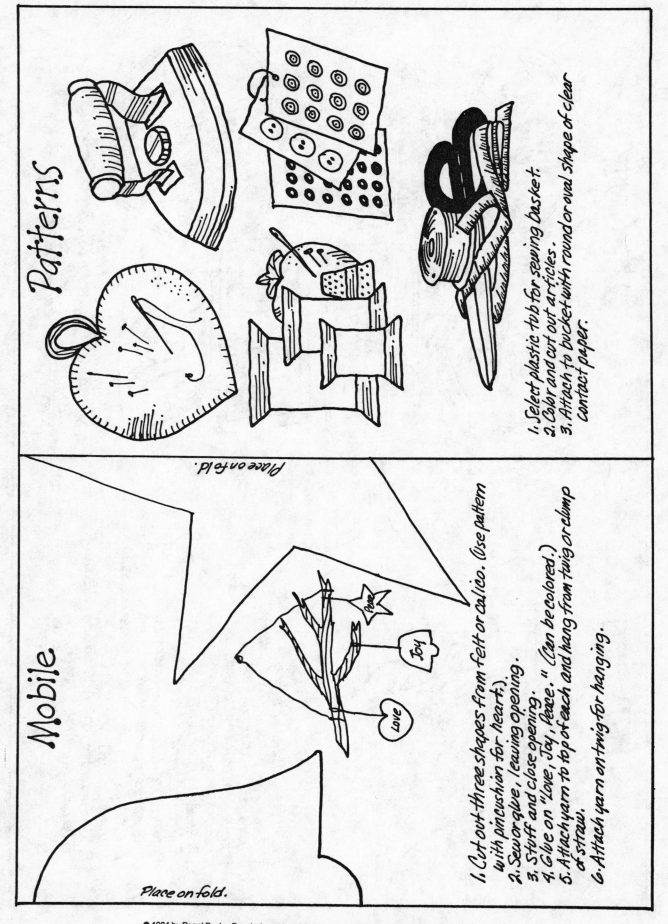

Patterns

1. Select plastic tub for sewing basket.
2. Color and cut out articles.
3. Attach to bucket with round or oval shape of clear contact paper.

Place on fold.

Mobile

Love   Joy   Peace

1. Cut out three shapes from felt or calico. (Use pattern with pincushion for heart.)
2. Sew or glue, leaving opening.
3. Stuff and close opening.
4. Glue on "Love, Joy, Peace." (Can be colored.)
5. Attach yarn to top of each and hang from twig or clump of straw.
6. Attach yarn on twig for hanging.

Place on fold.

27
THE POWER OF GOD'S WOMAN

Have a banner made with the title of the series and have it hanging behind the podium throughout the meetings.

Place mats: Use the pattern enclosed (see figure 26) in collage form for place mats. They can be printed in a variety of colors, or placed on different colored construction paper for each week. Let your imagination be your guide for this series!

Session 1: Use this occasion for an Everybody's Birthday Party, featuring the birthstones for each month. Perhaps a gift wrapping demonstration would be a good feature. Birthday cake is a must for refreshments.

Session 2: For an icebreaker, have the women share how their first childhood home was heated.
Ask the women to bring mittens to hang on a "mitten tree"—then send mittens to a children's home or mission.
We found a lady who owned a knitting machine, and she brought it to Spice of Life and partly made a cap before our very eyes. Then, she shared her testimony concerning how the Lord had freed her from fear.

Session 3: Have woman from each table bring three or four items in a grocery bag for a centerpiece. The price of each item should be on the bottom of the article. As an icebreaker, each lady is to estimate the total cost of the articles in the bag. The lady coming closest takes the bag home for a prize.
How about a silent auction—with articles that are brought the week before and placed on tables for browsing and bidding before the meeting begins?
Try a fashion show of outfits that have been purchased for under $10.00 (from garage sales, or home sewn).

Session 4: Use mirror tiles with open Bibles for table centers. Why not invite a beauty consultant from a Christian organization to demonstrate skin care or discuss the most appropriate colors for skin and hair color combinations?
A special time of singing or a guest soloist will make this meeting more significant.

Session 5: Everybody wears an apron!
Centerpieces can be cleanser cans with flowers poked into the holes on top. Place mats can be paper towels. Have several women come with household hints that are out of the ordinary! Or let someone become "Heloise" and do a skit on cleaning house.
Have available the InterVarsity booklet *My Heart Christ's Home.* Depending on your budget, these could be used for favors or prizes. One woman could give a 5-minute booklet report before a special prayer time.

Session 6: Let this be a Mother's Day celebration, regardless of the time of year! Let every woman bring a photo of her mother—and share one special memory of her growing-up years.
Interestingly enough, your state Mother of the Year is very possibly a Christian—invite her to share her experience with you. Or elect one of your own! and make her queen for the day.

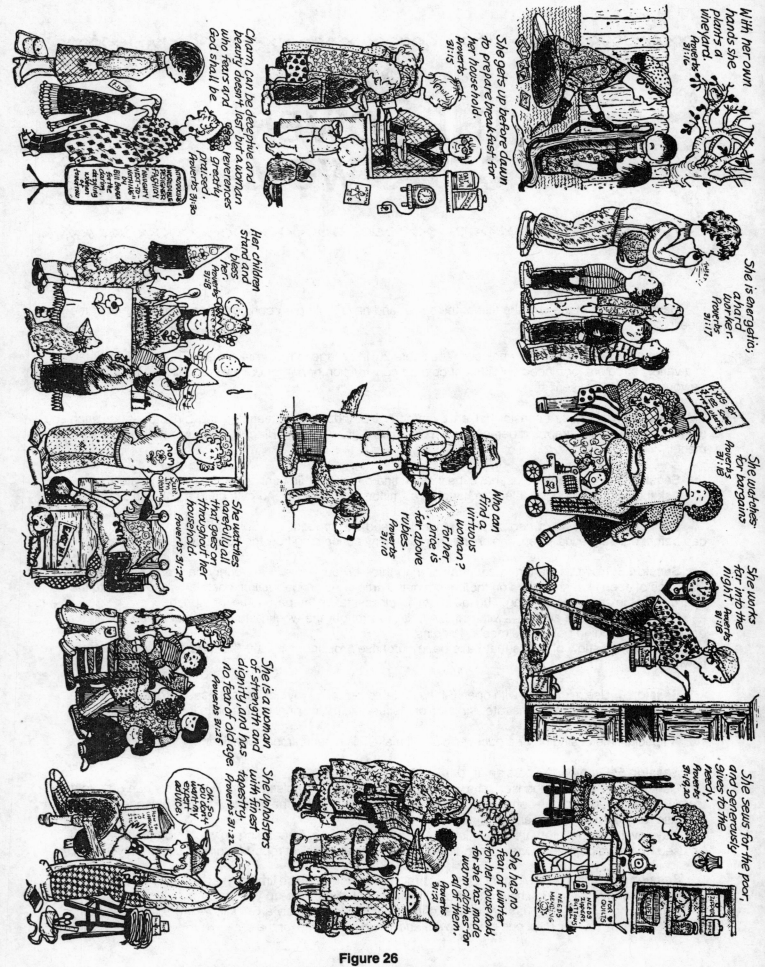

Figure 26

Session 7: This is the day to hear from the grandmothers. Or to invite every woman to bring a grand-mother with her—either her own or an adopted one. Let the older women "teach the younger women" through tips on homemaking, demonstrating a craft, devotional life, etc. Perhaps there is a senior citizens musical group that could offer a special selection or mini concert.

A few minutes of making some tray favors for a home for the aging would be time well spent.

Session 8: Hang fabric swatches around the room with numbered tags. Allow the women 5-10 minutes to try to identify the kind of fabrics and give some prizes appropriate to the day—a small woven bag, or pillow, needles, or sewing kit.

Use this day for a special time of worship, illustrating the fabrics and colors used in the Tabernacle.

Have a time of reflection on the life and ministry of Corrie ten Boom, with some of her books and photos displayed.

Session 9: Let everyone bring a plant slip for trading. Those women who exchange with one another become prayer partners.

Have grape juice to drink.

Use ivy plants for centerpieces. Even consider a field trip to a garden or a conservatory or an orchard.

Session 10: Why not a "Come as you are" breakfast?

Invite a nearby university, college, or 4H Club to come with a demonstration on eggs. Eat the product at your breakfast.

Session 11: Centerpieces could be kerosene lamps and clocks.

For an *icebreaker,* take time to have every woman move around the room and write in the squares (figure 27) the name of every lady each one talks to. Then ask one lady to call out one name which she has written on her square. As she does so, every woman who also has that name puts an *X* in the square. The woman whose name was called then calls out one she has on her square, and so on. The first woman who has five names in a line, either vertically, diagonally, or horizontally, wins the prize.

Session 12: Let the woman enter to the sounds of a Christian aerobics record. Invite them to wear sweatsuits for this occasion. Of course you will want to try some new and challenging exercises.

Session 13: Give your local mission a shower of clothing. Invite a representative from your local Salvation Army to report on their work in your community.

Have a day when some of your community service organizations are invited to make a display on card tables around the meeting room.

Plan a skit on James 1:2-9.

This is the day to inaugurate a special closet in the church for emergency clothing needs or a pantry of food.

Session 14: Your final week must be very special. We had a special contest to dress Mrs. Butterworth bottles like the woman pictures in Proverbs 31. These "ladies" were the centerpieces for our Mrs. Butterworth pancake brunch. Prizes were given for the cleverest, most beautiful, etc., etc.